MznLnx

Missing Links Exam Preps

Exam Prep for

Global Economic Issues and Policies

Daniels & VanHoose, 1st Edition

The MznLnx Exam Prep is your link from the texbook and lecture to your exams.
The MznLnx Exam Preps are unauthorized and comprehensive reviews of your textbooks.

All material provided by MznLnx and Rico Publications (c) 2010
Textbook publishers and textbook authors do not particpate in or contribute to these reviews.

MznLnx

Rico
Publications

Exam Prep for Global Economic Issues and Policies
1st Edition
Daniels & VanHoose

Publisher: Raymond Houge
Assistant Editor: Michael Rouger
Text and Cover Designer: Lisa Buckner
Marketing Manager: Sara Swagger
Project Manager, Editorial Production: Jerry Emerson
Art Director: Vernon Lowerui

Product Manager: Dave Mason
Editorial Assitant: Rachel Guzmanji
Pedagogy: Debra Long
Cover Image: Jim Reed/Getty Images
Text and Cover Printer: City Printing, Inc.
Compositor: Media Mix, Inc.

(c) 2010 Rico Publications

ALL RIGHTS RESERVED. No part of this work covered by the copyright may be reproduced or used in any form or by an means--graphic, electronic, or mechanical, including photocopying, recording, taping, Web distribution, information storage, and retrieval systems, or in any other manner--without the written permission of the publisher.

Printed in the United States
ISBN:

For more information about our products, contact us at:

Dave.Mason@RicoPublications.com

For permission to use material from this text or product, submit a request online to:

Dave.Mason@RicoPublications.com

Contents

CHAPTER 1
Understanding the Global Economy   1

CHAPTER 2
Comparative Advantage-How Nations Can Gain from International Trade   10

CHAPTER 3
Sources of Comparative Advantage   13

CHAPTER 4
Regulating International Trade-Trade Policies and Their Effects   22

CHAPTER 5
Regionalism and Multilateralism   27

CHAPTER 6
Balance of Payments and Foreign Exchange Markets   36

CHAPTER 7
Exchange-Rate Systems, Past to Present   50

CHAPTER 8
The Power of Arbitrage—Purchasing Power and Interest Rate Parities   62

CHAPTER 9
Global Money and Banking—Where Central Banks Fit into the World Economy   71

CHAPTER 10
Can Globalization Lift All Boats?   86

CHAPTER 11
Industrial Structure and Trade in the Global Economy Businesses without Borders   94

CHAPTER 12
The Public Sector in the Global Economy   105

CHAPTER 13
Rules versus Discretion—Can Policymakers Stick to Their Promises?   115

CHAPTER 14
Dealing with Financial Crises—Does   123

ANSWER KEY   131

TO THE STUDENT

COMPREHENSIVE

The *MznLnx* Exam Prep series is designed to help you pass your exams. Editors at MznLnx review your textbooks and then prepare these practice exams to help you master the textbook material. Unlike study guides, workbooks, and practice tests provided by the texbook publisher and textbook authors, *MznLnx* gives you **all** of the material in each chapter in exam form, not just samples, so you can be sure to nail your exam.

MECHANICAL

The MznLnx Exam Prep series creates exams that will help you learn the subject matter as well as test you on your understanding. Each question is designed to help you master the concept. Just working through the exams, you gain an understanding of the subject--its a simple mechanical process that produces success.

INTEGRATED STUDY GUIDE AND REVIEW

MznLnx is not just a set of exams designed to test you, its also a comprehensive review of the subject content. Each exam question is also a review of the concept, making sure that you will get the answer correct without having to go to other sources of material. You learn as you go! Its the easiest way to pass an exam.

HUMOR

Studying can be tedious and dry. MznLnx's instructional design includes moderate humor within the exam questions on occassion, to break the tedium and revitalize the brain

Chapter 1. Understanding the Global Economy 1

1. _____ was an international coalition movement in over 40 countries that called for cancellation of third world debt by the year 2000. This movement coincided with the Great Jubilee, the celebration of the year 2000 in the Catholic Church. From early 2001, _____ split into an array of organisations around the world.
   a. 130-30 fund
   b. 1921 recession
   c. Jubilee 2000
   d. 100-year flood

2. _____ in its literal sense is the process of transformation of local or regional phenomena into global ones. It can be described as a process by which the people of the world are unified into a single society and function together.

   This process is a combination of economic, technological, sociocultural and political forces.

   a. Helsinki Process on Globalisation and Democracy
   b. Global Cosmopolitanism
   c. Globally Integrated Enterprise
   d. Globalization

3. The _____ is where currency trading takes place. It is where banks and other official institutions facilitate the buying and selling of foreign currencies. FX transactions typically involve one party purchasing a quantity of one currency in exchange for paying a quantity of another.
   a. Foreign exchange market
   b. Currency swap
   c. Floating currency
   d. Covered interest arbitrage

4. _____s is the social science that studies the production, distribution, and consumption of goods and services. The term _____s comes from the Ancient Greek oá¼°κονομῖα from oá¼¶κος (oikos, 'house') + vÏŒμος (nomos, 'custom' or 'law'), hence 'rules of the house(hold)'. Current _____ models developed out of the broader field of political economy in the late 19th century, owing to a desire to use an empirical approach more akin to the physical sciences.
   a. Energy economics
   b. Opportunity cost
   c. Inflation
   d. Economic

5. _____ is a term used to describe how different aspects between economies are integrated. The basics of this theory were written by the Hungarian Economist Béla Balassa in the 1960s. As _____ increases, the barriers of trade between markets diminishes.

a. Import license
b. Inward investment
c. Import
d. Economic integration

6. A _____ is an object whose consumption increases the utility of the consumer, for which the quantity demanded exceeds the quantity supplied at zero price. _____s are usually modeled as having diminishing marginal utility. The first individual purchase has high utility; the second has less.
   a. Composite good
   b. Pie method
   c. Good
   d. Merit good

7. In economics, economic output is divided into physical goods and intangible services. Consumption of _____ is assumed to produce utility. It is often used when referring to a _____ Tax.
   a. Composite good
   b. Private good
   c. Manufactured goods
   d. Goods and services

8. In economics, a _____ is a mechanism that allows people to easily buy and sell (trade) financial securities (such as stocks and bonds), commodities (such as precious metals or agricultural goods), and other fungible items of value at low transaction costs and at prices that reflect the efficient-market hypothesis.

   _____s have evolved significantly over several hundred years and are undergoing constant innovation to improve liquidity.

   Both general markets (where many commodities are traded) and specialized markets (where only one commodity is traded) exist.

   a. Market anomaly
   b. Convertible arbitrage
   c. Financial market
   d. Noise trader

9. _____ in its classic form is defined as a company from one country making a physical investment into building a factory in another country. It is the establishment of an enterprise by a foreigner. Its definition can be extended to include investments made to acquire lasting interest in enterprises operating outside of the economy of the investor.

Chapter 1. Understanding the Global Economy   3

a. Financial Stability Forum
b. Federal Deposit Insurance Corporation
c. Foreign direct investment
d. Non-governmental organization

10. The _____ was established in 1964 as a permanent intergovernmental body. It is the principal organ of the United Nations General Assembly dealing with trade, investment and development issues.

The organization's goals are to 'maximize the trade, investment and development opportunities of developing countries and assist them in their efforts to integrate into the world economy on an equitable basis.' (from official website.)

a. Our Global Neighborhood
b. International Standards of Accounting and Reporting
c. International Trade Centre
d. United Nations Conference on Trade and Development

11. Economics:

- _____,the desire to own something and the ability to pay for it
- _____ curve,a graphic representation of a _____ schedule
- _____ deposit, the money in checking accounts
- _____ pull theory,the theory that inflation occurs when _____ for goods and services exceeds existing supplies
- _____ schedule,a table that lists the quantity of a good a person will buy it each different price
- _____ side economics,the school of economics at believes government spending and tax cuts open economy by raising _____

a. McKesson ' Robbins scandal
b. Variability
c. Production
d. Demand

12. _____ is an economic model based on price, utility and quantity in a market. It predicts that in a competitive market, price will function to equalize the quantity demanded by consumers, and the quantity supplied by producers, resulting in an economic equilibrium of price and quantity. The model incorporates other factors changing equilibrium as a shift of demand and/or supply.

a. Deferred gratification
b. Joint demand
c. Rational addiction
d. Supply and demand

13. In economics, a _____ is a table that lists the quantity of a good a person will buy it each different price See Demand curve.
   a. Rational irrationality
   b. Free contract
   c. Federal Reserve districts
   d. Demand schedule

14. In economics, the _____ is an economic law that states that consumers buy more of a good when its price decreases and less when its price increases.

There are certain goods which do not follow this law. These include Veblen and Giffen goods

   a. Market failure
   b. Financial crisis
   c. Georgism
   d. Law of demand

15. In economics, the _____ is the tendency of suppliers to offer more of a good at a higher price. The relationship between price and quantity supplied is usually a positive relationship. A rise in price is associated with a rise in quantity supplied.
   a. Mathematical economics
   b. Heterodox economics
   c. Market failure
   d. Law of supply

16. _____ refers to a business or organization attempting to acquire goods or services to accomplish the goals of the enterprise. Though there are several organizations that attempt to set standards in the _____ process, processes can vary greatly between organizations. Typically the word '_____' is not used interchangeably with the word 'procurement', since procurement typically includes Expediting, Supplier Quality, and Traffic and Logistics (T'L) in addition to _____.

a. Free port
b. 100-year flood
c. 130-30 fund
d. Purchasing

17. _____ is the number of goods/services that can be purchased with a unit of currency. For example, if you had taken one dollar to a store in the 1950s, you would have been able to buy a greater number of items than you would today, indicating that you would have had a greater _____ in the 1950s. Currency can be either a commodity money, like gold or silver, or fiat currency like US dollars.
    a. Human Poverty Index
    b. Genuine progress indicator
    c. Purchasing power
    d. Compliance cost

18. The _____ theory uses the long-term equilibrium exchange rate of two currencies to equalize their purchasing power. Developed by Gustav Cassel in 1920, it is based on the law of one price: the theory states that, in ideally efficient markets, identical goods should have only one price.

This purchasing power SEM rate equalizes the purchasing power of different currencies in their home countries for a given basket of goods.

    a. Measures of national income and output
    b. Gross national product
    c. Purchasing power parity
    d. Bureau of Labor Statistics

19. A _____ is a duty imposed on goods when they are moved across a political boundary. They are usually associated with protectionism, the economic policy of restraining trade between nations. For political reasons, _____s are usually imposed on imported goods, although they may also be imposed on exported goods.
    a. 1921 recession
    b. 130-30 fund
    c. Tariff
    d. 100-year flood

20. In economics, the _____ can be defined as the graph depicting the relationship between the price of a certain commodity, and the amount of it that consumers are willing and able to purchase at that given price. It is a graphic representation of a demand schedule. The _____ for all consumers together follows from the _____ of every individual consumer: the individual demands at each price are added together.

a. Kuznets curve
b. Wage curve
c. Cost curve
d. Demand curve

21. In consumer theory, an _____ is a good that decreases in demand when consumer income rises, unlike normal goods, for which the opposite is observed. It is a good that consumers demand increases when their income increases. Inferiority, in this sense, is an observable fact relating to affordability rather than a statement about the quality of the good.

    a. Inferior good
    b. Independent goods
    c. Information good
    d. Export-oriented

22. In economics, _____s are any goods for which demand increases when income increases and falls when income decreases but price remains constant, i.e. with a positive income elasticity of demand. The term does not necessarily refer to the quality of the good.

Depending on the indifference curves, the amount of a good bought can either increase, decrease, or stay the same when income increases.

    a. Financial contagion
    b. Normal good
    c. Bord halfpenny
    d. Normative economics

23. In economics, one kind of good (or service) is said to be a _____ for another kind in so far as the two kinds of goods can be consumed or used in place of one another in at least some of their possible uses.

Classic examples of _____s include margarine and butter, or petroleum and natural gas (used for heating or electricity.) The fact that one good is substitutable for another has immediate economic consequences: insofar as one good can be substituted for another, the demand for the two kinds of good will be bound together by the fact that customers can trade off one good for the other if it becomes advantageous to do so.

    a. Veblen goods
    b. Merit good
    c. Private good
    d. Substitute good

Chapter 1. Understanding the Global Economy

24. In economics, an _____ is any good or commodity, transported from one country to another country in a legitimate fashion, typically for use in trade. _____ goods or services are provided to foreign consumers by domestic producers. _____ is an important part of international trade.
   a. ACCRA Cost of Living Index
   b. ACEA agreement
   c. AD-IA Model
   d. Export

25. In microeconomics, _____ is quite simply the conversion of inputs into outputs. It is an economic process that uses resources to create a good or service that is suitable for exchange. This can include manufacturing, storing, shipping, and packaging.
   a. Solved
   b. Red Guards
   c. MET
   d. Production

26. _____ is a broad label that refers to any individuals or households that use goods and services generated within the economy. The concept of a _____ is used in different contexts, so that the usage and significance of the term may vary.

Typically when business people and economists talk of _____s they are talking about person as _____, an aggregated commodity item with little individuality other than that expressed in the buy/not-buy decision.

   a. 1921 recession
   b. Consumer
   c. 100-year flood
   d. 130-30 fund

27. The term surplus is used in economics for several related quantities. The _____ is the amount that consumers benefit by being able to purchase a product for a price that is less than they would be willing to pay. The producer surplus is the amount that producers benefit by selling at a market price mechanism that is higher than they would be willing to sell for.
   a. Necessity good
   b. Consumer surplus
   c. Microeconomic reform
   d. Marginal rate of technical substitution

Chapter 1. Understanding the Global Economy

28. The term surplus is used in economics for several related quantities. The consumer surplus is the amount that consumers benefit by being able to purchase a product for a price that is less than they would be willing to pay. The _____ is the amount that producers benefit by selling at a market price mechanism that is higher than they would be willing to sell for.
    a. Long term
    b. Returns to scale
    c. Schedule delay
    d. Producer surplus

29. _____ is an economic concept with commonplace familiarity. It is the price that a good or service is offered at, or will fetch, in the marketplace. It is of interest mainly in the study of microeconomics.
    a. Market anomaly
    b. Market price
    c. Paper trading
    d. Noisy market hypothesis

30. _____ in economics and business is the result of an exchange and from that trade we assign a numerical monetary value to a good, service or asset. If Alice trades Bob 4 apples for an orange, the _____ of an orange is 4 apples. Inversely, the _____ of an apple is 1/4 oranges.
    a. Premium pricing
    b. Price war
    c. Price book
    d. Price

31. In economics, _____ refers to either

    1. a simplifying assumption made by the new classical school that markets always go to where the quantity supplied equals the quantity demanded; or
    2. the process of getting there via price adjustment.

A _____ price is the price of a good or service at which quantity supplied is equal to quantity demanded. Also called the equilibrium price.

In simple terms, this means that markets tend to move towards prices which balance the quantity supplied and the quantity demanded, such that the market will eventually be cleared of all surpluses and shortages (excess supply and demand.) The first version assumes that this process occurs instantaneously.

a. Market portfolio
b. Market data
c. Noise trader
d. Market clearing

32. In economics, an _____ is any good (e.g. a commodity) or service brought into one country from another country in a legitimate fashion, typically for use in trade. It is a good that is brought in from another country for sale. _____ goods or services are provided to domestic consumers by foreign producers. An _____ in the receiving country is an export to the sending country.
    a. Incoterms
    b. Import quota
    c. Economic integration
    d. Import

Chapter 2. Comparative Advantage-How Nations Can Gain from International Trade

1. An _____ is an economy that is self-sufficient and does not take part in international trade, or severely limits trade with the outside world. Likewise the term refers to an ecosystem not affected by influences from the outside, which relies entirely on its own resources. In the economic meaning, it is also referred to as a closed economy.

    a. Autarky
    b. Attention work
    c. Internet Economy
    d. Underground economy

2. In microeconomics, _____ is quite simply the conversion of inputs into outputs. It is an economic process that uses resources to create a good or service that is suitable for exchange. This can include manufacturing, storing, shipping, and packaging.

    a. MET
    b. Solved
    c. Red Guards
    d. Production

3. In economics, _____ refers to the ability of a party to produce a good or service using fewer real resources than another entity producing the same good or service..A party has an _____ when using the same input as another party, it can produce a greater output. Since _____ is determined by a simple comparison of labor productivities, it is possible for a a party to have no _____ in anything. It can be contrasted with the concept of comparative advantage which refers to the ability to produce a particular good at a lower opportunity cost.

    a. Absolute advantage
    b. International economics
    c. Index number
    d. ACCRA Cost of Living Index

4. _____s is the social science that studies the production, distribution, and consumption of goods and services. The term _____s comes from the Ancient Greek οἰκονομῐ́α from οἶκος (oikos, 'house') + νόμος (nomos, 'custom' or 'law'), hence 'rules of the house(hold)'. Current _____ models developed out of the broader field of political economy in the late 19th century, owing to a desire to use an empirical approach more akin to the physical sciences.

    a. Economic
    b. Inflation
    c. Energy economics
    d. Opportunity cost

5. _____ or economic opportunity loss is the value of the next best alternative foregone as the result of making a decision. _____ analysis is an important part of a company's decision-making processes but is not treated as an actual cost in any financial statement. The next best thing that a person can engage in is referred to as the _____ of doing the best thing and ignoring the next best thing to be done.

a. Opportunity cost
b. Economic ideology
c. Economic
d. Industrial organization

6. _____ is a common concept in economics, and gives rise to derived concepts such as consumer debt. Generally _____ is defined by opposition to production. But the precise definition can vary because different schools of economists define production quite differently.
   a. Federal Reserve Bank Notes
   b. Cash or share options
   c. Foreclosure data providers
   d. Consumption

7. In economics, _____ refers to the ability of a person or a country to produce a particular good at a lower marginal cost and opportunity cost than another person or country. It is the ability to produce a product most efficiently given all the other products that could be produced. It can be contrasted with absolute advantage which refers to the ability of a person or a country to produce a particular good at a lower absolute cost than another.
   a. Hot money
   b. Triffin dilemma
   c. Comparative advantage
   d. Gravity model of trade

8. _____ is the advantage gained by the initial occupant of a market segment. This advantage may stem from the fact that the first entrant can gain control of resources that followers may not be able to match. Sometimes the first mover is not able to capitalise on its advantage, leaving the opportunity for another firm to gain second-mover advantage.
   a. First-mover advantage
   b. Business engineering
   c. Cross-docking
   d. Continuous Improvement Process

9. A _____ is the procedure of systematically acquiring and recording information about the members of a given population. It is a regularly occurring and official count of a particular population. The term is used mostly in connection with national 'population and door to door _____es' (to be taken every 10 years according to United Nations recommendations), agriculture, and business _____es.

a. 100-year flood
b. 130-30 fund
c. 1921 recession
d. Census

Chapter 3. Sources of Comparative Advantage

1. _____ is a type of trade policy that allows traders to act and transact without interference from government. Thus, the policy permits trading partners mutual gains from trade, with goods and services produced according to the theory of comparative advantage.

Under a _____ policy, prices are a reflection of true supply and demand, and are the sole determinant of resource allocation.

   a. 100-year flood
   b. 1921 recession
   c. Free Trade
   d. 130-30 fund

2. The _____ is a trilateral trade bloc in North America created by the governments of the United States, Canada, and Mexico. The agreement creating the trade bloc came into force on January 1, 1994. It superseded the Canada-United States Free Trade Agreement between the U.S. and Canada.
   a. Federal Reserve Bank Notes
   b. Case-Shiller Home Price Indices
   c. Demand-side technologies
   d. North American Free Trade Agreement

3. A _____ is a duty imposed on goods when they are moved across a political boundary. They are usually associated with protectionism, the economic policy of restraining trade between nations. For political reasons, _____s are usually imposed on imported goods, although they may also be imposed on exported goods.
   a. 100-year flood
   b. 130-30 fund
   c. 1921 recession
   d. Tariff

Chapter 3. Sources of Comparative Advantage

4. A _____ is a general term that describes any government policy or regulation that restricts international trade. The barriers can take many forms, including the following terms that include many restrictions in international trade within multiple countries that import and export any items of trade.

- Import duty
- Import licenses
- Export licenses
- Import quotas
- Tariffs
- Subsidies
- Non-tariff barriers to trade
- Voluntary Export Restraints
- Local Content Requirements
- Embargo

Most _____s work on the same principle: the imposition of some sort of cost on trade that raises the price of the traded products. If two or more nations repeatedly use _____s against each other, then a trade war results.

a. National Foreign Trade Council
b. Trade barrier
c. Certificate of origin
d. Global financial system

5. In economics, _____ are the resources employed to produce goods and services. They facilitate production but do not become part of the product (as with raw materials) or significantly transformed by the production process (as with fuel used to power machinery.) To 19th century economists, the _____ were land (natural resources, gifts from nature), labor (the ability to work), and capital goods (human-made tools and equipment.)

a. Factors of production
b. Hicks-neutral technical change
c. Product Pipeline
d. Long-run

6. In microeconomics, _____ is quite simply the conversion of inputs into outputs. It is an economic process that uses resources to create a good or service that is suitable for exchange. This can include manufacturing, storing, shipping, and packaging.

a. Red Guards
b. Solved
c. MET
d. Production

Chapter 3. Sources of Comparative Advantage

7. In economics a country's _____ is commonly understood as the amount of land, labor, capital, and entrepreneurship that a country possesses and can exploit for manufacturing. Countries with a large endowment of resources tend to be more prosperous than those with a small endowment, all other things being equal. The development of sound institutions to access and equitably distribute these resources, however, is necessary in order for a country to obtain the greatest benefit from its _____.

   a. Foreign Affiliate Trade Statistics
   b. Dutch disease
   c. Price scissors
   d. Factor endowment

8. A _____ is an object whose consumption increases the utility of the consumer, for which the quantity demanded exceeds the quantity supplied at zero price. _____s are usually modeled as having diminishing marginal utility. The first individual purchase has high utility; the second has less.

   a. Pie method
   b. Good
   c. Composite good
   d. Merit good

9. The _____ is one of the four critical theorems of the Heckscher-Ohlin model. It states: 'A capital-abundant country will export the capital-intensive good, while the labor-abundant country will export the labor-intensive good.'

The critical assumption of the Heckscher-Ohlin model is that the two countries are identical, except for the difference in resource endowments. This also implies that the aggregate preferences are the same.

   a. No-trade theorem
   b. 100-year flood
   c. Stolper-Samuelson theorem
   d. Heckscher-Ohlin theorem

10. In economics, _____ refers to the ability of a party to produce a good or service using fewer real resources than another entity producing the same good or service..A party has an _____ when using the same input as another party, it can produce a greater output. Since _____ is determined by a simple comparison of labor productivities, it is possible for a a party to have no _____ in anything. It can be contrasted with the concept of comparative advantage which refers to the ability to produce a particular good at a lower opportunity cost.

   a. Absolute advantage
   b. Index number
   c. ACCRA Cost of Living Index
   d. International economics

Chapter 3. Sources of Comparative Advantage

11. An _____ is an economy that is self-sufficient and does not take part in international trade, or severely limits trade with the outside world. Likewise the term refers to an ecosystem not affected by influences from the outside, which relies entirely on its own resources. In the economic meaning, it is also referred to as a closed economy.
    a. Internet Economy
    b. Autarky
    c. Underground economy
    d. Attention work

12. In economics, economic output is divided into physical goods and intangible services. Consumption of _____ is assumed to produce utility. It is often used when referring to a _____ Tax.
    a. Goods and services
    b. Manufactured goods
    c. Private good
    d. Composite good

13. The _____ is the apparent contradiction that although water is on the whole more useful, in terms of survival, than diamonds, diamonds command a higher price in the market. The economist Adam Smith is often considered to be the classic presenter of this paradox. Nicolaus Copernicus, John Locke, John Law and others had previously tried to explain the disparity.
    a. 100-year flood
    b. St. Petersburg paradox
    c. 130-30 fund
    d. Paradox of value

14. _____s is the social science that studies the production, distribution, and consumption of goods and services. The term _____s comes from the Ancient Greek οἰκονομία from οἶκος (oikos, 'house') + νόμος (nomos, 'custom' or 'law'), hence 'rules of the house(hold)'. Current _____ models developed out of the broader field of political economy in the late 19th century, owing to a desire to use an empirical approach more akin to the physical sciences.
    a. Energy economics
    b. Opportunity cost
    c. Inflation
    d. Economic

15. A _____ is an expression that compares quantities relative to each other. The most common examples involve two quantities, but any number of quantities can be compared. _____s are represented mathematically by separating each quantity with a colon, for example the _____ 2:3, which is read as the _____ 'two to three'.

a. Ratio
b. 100-year flood
c. 130-30 fund
d. Y-intercept

16. _____ refers to the stock of skills and knowledge embodied in the ability to perform labor so as to produce economic value. It is the skills and knowledge gained by a worker through education and experience. Many early economic theories refer to it simply as labor, one of three factors of production, and consider it to be a fungible resource -- homogeneous and easily interchangeable. Other conceptions of labor dispense with these assumptions.

a. Law of increasing costs
b. General equilibrium
c. Price theory
d. Human capital

17. _____ are the prices that the factors of production of a finished item attract.

There has been some economic debate as to what determines these prices. Classical and Marxist economists argued that the _____ decided the value of a product and so value was intrinsic within the product.

a. Marginal product
b. Marginal product of labor
c. Productivity model
d. Factor prices

18. _____ is an economic theory, which states that the relative prices for two identical factors of production in the same market will eventually equal each other because of competition. The price for each single factor need not become equal, but relative factors will. Whichever factor receives the lowest price before two countries integrate economically and effectively become one market will therefore tend to become more expensive relative to other factors in the economy, while those with the highest price will tend to become cheaper.

a. Premium pricing
b. Price book
c. Big ticket item
d. Factor price equalization

19. _____ in economics and business is the result of an exchange and from that trade we assign a numerical monetary value to a good, service or asset. If Alice trades Bob 4 apples for an orange, the _____ of an orange is 4 apples. Inversely, the _____ of an apple is 1/4 oranges.

Chapter 3. Sources of Comparative Advantage

   a. Premium pricing
   b. Price
   c. Price book
   d. Price war

20. _____ is the income of individuals or nations after adjusting for inflation. It is calculated by subtracting inflation from the nominal income. Real variables, such as _____, real GDP, and real interest rate are variables that are measured in physical units, while nominal variables such as nominal income, nominal GDP, and nominal interest rate are measured in monetary units.
   a. Real income
   b. Family income
   c. Windfall gain
   d. Net national income

21. The _____ is a specialized agency of the United Nations that deals with labour issues. Its headquarters are in Geneva, Switzerland. Its secretariat -- the people who are employed by it throughout the world -- is known as the International Labour Office.
   a. International Labour Organization
   b. AD-IA Model
   c. ACCRA Cost of Living Index
   d. ACEA agreement

22. The _____ is a basic theorem in trade theory. It describes a relation between the relative prices of output goods and relative factor rewards, specifically, real wages and real returns to capital.

The theorem states that -- under some economic assumptions (constant returns, perfect competition) -- a rise in the relative price of a good will lead to a rise in the return to that factor which is used most intensively in the production of the good, and conversely, to a fall in the return to the other factor.

   a. No-trade theorem
   b. 100-year flood
   c. Stolper-Samuelson theorem
   d. Heckscher-Ohlin theorem

23. In economics, _____ refers to the ability of a person or a country to produce a particular good at a lower marginal cost and opportunity cost than another person or country. It is the ability to produce a product most efficiently given all the other products that could be produced. It can be contrasted with absolute advantage which refers to the ability of a person or a country to produce a particular good at a lower absolute cost than another.

Chapter 3. Sources of Comparative Advantage

a. Hot money
b. Triffin dilemma
c. Comparative advantage
d. Gravity model of trade

24. A contract manufacturer ('_____') is a firm that manufactures components or products for another 'hiring' firm. Many industries utilize this process, especially the aerospace, defense, computer, semiconductor, energy, medical, food manufacturing, personal care, and automotive fields. Some types of _____ include CNC machining, complex assembly, aluminum die casting, grinding, broaching, gears, and forging.
    a. Marginal rate of transformation
    b. Contract manufacturing
    c. Production-possibility frontier
    d. Piece work

25. _____ is exchange of capital, goods, and services across international borders or territories. In most countries, it represents a significant share of gross domestic product (GDP.) While _____ has been present throughout much of history, its economic, social, and political importance has been on the rise in recent centuries.
    a. Import license
    b. Incoterms
    c. Intra-industry trade
    d. International trade

26. _____ is subcontracting a process, such as product design or manufacturing, to a third-party company. The decision to outsource is often made in the interest of lowering cost or making better use of time and energy costs, redirecting or conserving energy directed at the competencies of a particular business, or to make more efficient use of land, labor, capital, (information) technology and resources. _____ became part of the business lexicon during the 1980s.
    a. Additional Funds Needed
    b. Electronic business
    c. Averch-Johnson effect
    d. Outsourcing

27. _____ is the a method of technical and economic research of the systems for purpose to optimize a parity between system's consumer functions or properties and expenses to achieve those functions or properties.

Chapter 3. Sources of Comparative Advantage

This methodology for continuous perfection of production, industrial technologies, organizational structures was developed by Juryj Sobolev in 1948 at the 'Perm telephone factory'

- 1948 Juryj Sobolev - the first success in application of a method analysis at the 'Perm telephone factory'.
- 1949 - the first application for the invention as result of use of the new method.

Today in economically developed countries practically each enterprise or the company use methodology of the kind of functional-cost analysis as a practice of the quality management, most full satisfying to principles of standards of series ISO 9000.

- Interest of consumer not in products itself, but the advantage which it will receive from its usage.
- The consumer aspires to reduce his expenses
- Functions needed by consumer can be executed in the various ways, and, hence, with various efficiency and expenses. Among possible alternatives of realization of functions exist such in which the parity of quality and the price is the optimal for the consumer.

The goal of _____ is achievement of the highest consumer satisfaction of production at simultaneous decrease in all kinds of industrial expenses Classical _____ has three English synonyms - Value Engineering, Value Management, Value Analysis.

  a. Willingness to pay
  b. Function cost analysis
  c. Staple financing
  d. Monopoly wage

28. _____ refers to the additional value of a commodity over the cost of commodities used to produce it from the previous stage of production. An example is the price of gasoline at the pump over the price of the oil in it. In national accounts used in macroeconomics, it refers to the contribution of the factors of production, i.e., land, labor, and capital goods, to raising the value of a product and corresponds to the incomes received by the owners of these factors.
  a. Full employment
  b. Value added
  c. Solow residual
  d. Hodrick-Prescott filter

29. _____ has been viewed as a process of increasing involvement of enterprises in international markets, although there is no agreed definition of _____ or international entrepreneurship. There are several _____ theories which try to explain why there are international activities.

Adam Smith claimed that a country should specialise in, and export, commodities in which it had an absolute advantage.

a. Economic problem
b. Uppsala model
c. Unified growth theory
d. Internationalization

30. _____ is the increase in the amount of the goods and services produced by an economy over time. It is conventionally measured as the percent rate of increase in real gross domestic product, or real GDP. Growth is usually calculated in real terms, i.e. inflation-adjusted terms, in order to net out the effect of inflation on the price of the goods and services produced.

a. AD-IA Model
b. ACCRA Cost of Living Index
c. Economic growth
d. ACEA agreement

31. Founded in 1991, the _____ uses the tools of investment to help build market economies and democracies in 27 countries from central Europe to central Asia. Its mission was to support the formerly communist countries in the process of establishing their private sectors.

Headquartered in London, the EBRD is owned by 61 countries and two intergovernmental institutions.

a. ACCRA Cost of Living Index
b. AD-IA Model
c. European Bank for Reconstruction and Development
d. ACEA agreement

32. The _____ is an important selective, mainly private, international organization designed by its founders to supervise and liberalize international trade. The organization officially commenced on 1 January 1995, under the Marrakesh Agreement, succeeding the 1947 General Agreement on Tariffs and Trade (GATT.)

The _____ deals with regulation of trade between participating countries; it provides a framework for negotiating and formalising trade agreements, and a dispute resolution process aimed at enforcing participants' adherence to _____ agreements which are signed by representatives of member governments and ratified by their parliaments.

a. 2009 G-20 London summit protests
b. Backus-Kehoe-Kydland consumption correlation puzzle
c. Bio-energy village
d. World Trade Organization

Chapter 4. Regulating International Trade-Trade Policies and Their Effects

1. _____ is a term in international relations that refers to multiple countries working in concert on a given issue.

Most international organizations, such as the United Nations (UN) and the World Trade Organization are multilateral in nature. The main proponents of _____ have traditionally been the middle powers such as Canada, Australia and the Nordic countries.

   a. Simultaneous policy
   b. 100-year flood
   c. Global governance
   d. Multilateralism

2. A _____ is a general term that describes any government policy or regulation that restricts international trade. The barriers can take many forms, including the following terms that include many restrictions in international trade within multiple countries that import and export any items of trade.

   - Import duty
   - Import licenses
   - Export licenses
   - Import quotas
   - Tariffs
   - Subsidies
   - Non-tariff barriers to trade
   - Voluntary Export Restraints
   - Local Content Requirements
   - Embargo

Most _____s work on the same principle: the imposition of some sort of cost on trade that raises the price of the traded products. If two or more nations repeatedly use _____s against each other, then a trade war results.

   a. Global financial system
   b. Trade barrier
   c. Certificate of origin
   d. National Foreign Trade Council

3. A _____ is a duty imposed on goods when they are moved across a political boundary. They are usually associated with protectionism, the economic policy of restraining trade between nations. For political reasons, _____s are usually imposed on imported goods, although they may also be imposed on exported goods.

Chapter 4. Regulating International Trade-Trade Policies and Their Effects

a. 130-30 fund
b. Tariff
c. 1921 recession
d. 100-year flood

4. To _____ is to impose a financial charge or other levy upon a taxpayer by a state or the functional equivalent of a state.

_____es are also imposed by many subnational entities. _____es consist of direct _____ or indirect _____, and may be paid in money or as its labour equivalent (often but not always unpaid.)

a. 130-30 fund
b. 1921 recession
c. 100-year flood
d. Tax

5. To tax is to impose a financial charge or other levy upon a taxpayer by a state or the functional equivalent of a state.

_____ are also imposed by many subnational entities. _____ consist of direct tax or indirect tax, and may be paid in money or as its labour equivalent (often but not always unpaid.)

a. 1921 recession
b. 100-year flood
c. Taxes
d. 130-30 fund

6. _____ in economics and business is the result of an exchange and from that trade we assign a numerical monetary value to a good, service or asset. If Alice trades Bob 4 apples for an orange, the _____ of an orange is 4 apples. Inversely, the _____ of an apple is 1/4 oranges.
a. Price book
b. Price war
c. Premium pricing
d. Price

7. In economics, an _____ is any good or commodity, transported from one country to another country in a legitimate fashion, typically for use in trade. _____ goods or services are provided to foreign consumers by domestic producers. _____ is an important part of international trade.

Chapter 4. Regulating International Trade-Trade Policies and Their Effects

a. AD-IA Model
b. Export
c. ACCRA Cost of Living Index
d. ACEA agreement

8. In economics, _____ refers to the ability of a party to produce a good or service using fewer real resources than another entity producing the same good or service..A party has an _____ when using the same input as another party, it can produce a greater output. Since _____ is determined by a simple comparison of labor productivities, it is possible for a a party to have no _____ in anything. It can be contrasted with the concept of comparative advantage which refers to the ability to produce a particular good at a lower opportunity cost.

a. International economics
b. ACCRA Cost of Living Index
c. Absolute advantage
d. Index number

9. _____ is exchange of capital, goods, and services across international borders or territories. In most countries, it represents a significant share of gross domestic product (GDP.) While _____ has been present throughout much of history, its economic, social, and political importance has been on the rise in recent centuries.

a. Intra-industry trade
b. Incoterms
c. Import license
d. International Trade

10. In economics, a _____ is a loss of economic efficiency that can occur when equilibrium for a good or service is not Pareto optimal. In other words, either people who would have more marginal benefit than marginal cost are not buying the good or service, or people who would have more marginal cost than marginal benefit are buying the product.

Causes of _____ can include monopoly pricing, externalities, taxes or subsidies, and binding price ceilings or floors.

a. Contract curve
b. Deadweight loss
c. Leapfrogging
d. Distributive efficiency

Chapter 4. Regulating International Trade-Trade Policies and Their Effects 25

11. _____s is the social science that studies the production, distribution, and consumption of goods and services. The term _____s comes from the Ancient Greek oá¼°κονομῖα from oá¼¶κος (oikos, 'house') + vÏŒμος (nomos, 'custom' or 'law'), hence 'rules of the house(hold)'. Current _____ models developed out of the broader field of political economy in the late 19th century, owing to a desire to use an empirical approach more akin to the physical sciences.
   a. Inflation
   b. Opportunity cost
   c. Energy economics
   d. Economic

12. _____ is used to refer to a number of related concepts. It is the using resources in such a way as to maximize the production of goods and services. A system can be called economically efficient if:

   - No one can be made better off without making someone else worse off.
   - More output cannot be obtained without increasing the amount of inputs.
   - Production proceeds at the lowest possible per-unit cost.

   These definitions of efficiency are not equivalent, but they are all encompassed by the idea that nothing more can be achieved given the resources available.

   An economic system is more efficient if it can provide more goods and services for society without using more resources.

   a. ACCRA Cost of Living Index
   b. ACEA agreement
   c. Efficient contract theory
   d. Economic efficiency

13. In economics, an _____ is any good (e.g. a commodity) or service brought into one country from another country in a legitimate fashion, typically for use in trade. It is a good that is brought in from another country for sale. _____ goods or services are provided to domestic consumers by foreign producers. An _____ in the receiving country is an export to the sending country.
   a. Incoterms
   b. Economic integration
   c. Import quota
   d. Import

14. An _____ is a type of protectionist trade restriction that sets a physical limit on the quantity of a good that can be imported into a country in a given period of time. Quotas, like other trade restrictions, are used to benefit the producers of a good in a domestic economy at the expense of all consumers of the good in that economy.

Critics say quotas often lead to corruption (bribes to get a quota allocation), smuggling (circumventing a quota), and higher prices for consumers.

a. Import quota
b. Economic integration
c. Agreement on Agriculture
d. International Monetary Systems

15. Economic _____ is defined as an excess distribution to any factor in a production process above that which is required to induce the factor into the process or any excess above that which is necessary to keep the factor in its current use..

Classical Factor _____ is primarily concerned with the fee paid for the use of fixed (e.g. natural) resources. The classical definition is expressed as any excess payment above that required to induce or provide for production.

a. 1921 recession
b. 100-year flood
c. Rent
d. 130-30 fund

16. _____ are duties imposed under WTO Rules to neutralize the negative effects of other duties. They are imposed when a foreign country subsidizes its exports, hurting domestic producers in the importing country

a. Certificate of origin
b. Kennedy Round
c. Market access
d. Countervailing duties

Chapter 5. Regionalism and Multilateralism

1. _____ is sometimes referred to as _____, actually it means Economic Monetary Union.

First ideas of an economic and monetary union in Europe were raised well before establishing the European Communities. For example, already in the League of Nations, Gustav Stresemann asked in 1929 for a European currency (Link) against the background of an increased economic division due to a number of new nation states in Europe after WWI.

   a. Euro Interbank Offered Rate
   b. European Monetary System
   c. Exchange rate mechanism
   d. European Monetary Union

2. _____ is a type of trade policy that allows traders to act and transact without interference from government. Thus, the policy permits trading partners mutual gains from trade, with goods and services produced according to the theory of comparative advantage.

Under a _____ policy, prices are a reflection of true supply and demand, and are the sole determinant of resource allocation.

   a. 100-year flood
   b. 1921 recession
   c. 130-30 fund
   d. Free Trade

3. An economic and _____ is a single market with a common currency. It is to be distinguished from a mere currency union , which does not involve a single market. This is the fifth stage of economic integration.
   a. Commercial invoice
   b. Customs union
   c. Free trade zone
   d. Monetary Union

4. The _____ is a trilateral trade bloc in North America created by the governments of the United States, Canada, and Mexico. The agreement creating the trade bloc came into force on January 1, 1994. It superseded the Canada-United States Free Trade Agreement between the U.S. and Canada.
   a. Demand-side technologies
   b. Federal Reserve Bank Notes
   c. Case-Shiller Home Price Indices
   d. North American Free Trade Agreement

Chapter 5. Regionalism and Multilateralism

5. A _____ is a customs union with common policies on product regulation, and freedom of movement of the factors of production (capital and labour) and of enterprise. The goal is that the movement of capital, labour, goods, and services between the members is as easy as within them. This is the fourth stage of economic integration.
   a. Mutual recognition agreement
   b. Grey market
   c. Competitiveness
   d. Common market

6. A _____ is a free trade area with a common external tariff. The participant countries set up common external trade policy, but in some cases they use different import quotas. Common competition policy is also helpful to avoid competition deficiency.
   a. Grey market
   b. Bilateral Investment Treaty
   c. Customs union
   d. Common market

7. _____s is the social science that studies the production, distribution, and consumption of goods and services. The term _____s comes from the Ancient Greek oá¼°κονομῖα from oá¼¶κος (oikos, 'house') + vÏŒμος (nomos, 'custom' or 'law'), hence 'rules of the house(hold)'. Current _____ models developed out of the broader field of political economy in the late 19th century, owing to a desire to use an empirical approach more akin to the physical sciences.
   a. Energy economics
   b. Opportunity cost
   c. Economic
   d. Inflation

8. _____ is a designated group of countries that have agreed to eliminate tariffs, quotas and preferences on most (if not all) goods and services traded between them. It can be considered the second stage of economic integration. Countries choose this kind of economic integration form if their economical structures are complementary.
   a. 100-year flood
   b. 130-30 fund
   c. MERCOSUR
   d. Free trade area

9. In economics, _____ refers to the ability of a party to produce a good or service using fewer real resources than another entity producing the same good or service..A party has an _____ when using the same input as another party, it can produce a greater output. Since _____ is determined by a simple comparison of labor productivities, it is possible for a party to have no _____ in anything. It can be contrasted with the concept of comparative advantage which refers to the ability to produce a particular good at a lower opportunity cost.

a. Absolute advantage
b. Index number
c. ACCRA Cost of Living Index
d. International economics

10. A _____ or labor union is an organization of workers who have banded together to achieve common goals in key areas and working conditions. The _____, through its leadership, bargains with the employer on behalf of union members (rank and file members) and negotiates labor contracts (Collective bargaining) with employers. This may include the negotiation of wages, work rules, complaint procedures, rules governing hiring, firing and promotion of workers, benefits, workplace safety and policies.
a. Case-Shiller Home Price Indices
b. Trade union
c. Guaranteed investment contracts
d. Consumer goods

11. In economics, the _____ of an industry is used as an indicator of the relative size of firms in relation to the industry as a whole. It is calculated as the sum of the percent market share of the top n industries. This may also assist in determining the market structure of the industry.
a. Pacman conjecture
b. Concentration ratio
c. Monopolization
d. Quasi-rent

12. A _____ is an expression that compares quantities relative to each other. The most common examples involve two quantities, but any number of quantities can be compared. _____s are represented mathematically by separating each quantity with a colon, for example the _____ 2:3, which is read as the _____ 'two to three'.
a. Y-intercept
b. Ratio
c. 100-year flood
d. 130-30 fund

13. The _____ was a unilateral and temporary United States program initiated by the 1983 'Caribbean Basin Economic Recovery Act' (CBERA.) The _____ came into effect on January 1, 1984 and aimed to provide several tariff and trade benefits to many Central American and Caribbean countries. It arose in the context of a U.S. desire to respond with aid and trade to leftist movements that were active in some countries of the region, such as the guerrillas in El Salvador and the Sandinista government in Nicaragua.

Chapter 5. Regionalism and Multilateralism

   a. 130-30 fund
   b. 1921 recession
   c. 100-year flood
   d. Caribbean Basin Initiative

14. Asia-Pacific Economic Cooperation is a forum for 21 Pacific Rim countries (styled 'member economies') to cooperate on regional trade and investment liberalisation and facilitation. _____'s objective is to enhance economic growth and prosperity in the region and to strengthen the Asia-Pacific community. Members account for approximately 40% of the world's population, approximately 54% of world GDP and about 44% of world trade.
   a. Asia Pacific Economic Cooperation
   b. ACCRA Cost of Living Index
   c. AD-IA Model
   d. ACEA agreement

15. Founded in 1991, the _____ uses the tools of investment to help build market economies and democracies in 27 countries from central Europe to central Asia. Its mission was to support the formerly communist countries in the process of establishing their private sectors.

Headquartered in London, the EBRD is owned by 61 countries and two intergovernmental institutions.

   a. ACEA agreement
   b. European Bank for Reconstruction and Development
   c. AD-IA Model
   d. ACCRA Cost of Living Index

16. The _____ are two of the treaties of the European Union signed on March 25, 1957. Both treaties were signed by The Six: Belgium, France, Italy, Luxembourg, the Netherlands and West Germany.

The first established the European Economic Community and the second established the European Atomic Energy Community (EAEC or Euratom.)

   a. Treaties of Rome
   b. Maastricht Treaty
   c. 100-year flood
   d. Treaty of Amsterdam

Chapter 5. Regionalism and Multilateralism

17. The _____ is an economic and political union of 27 member states, located primarily in Europe. It was established by the Treaty of Maastricht on 1 November 1993, upon the foundations of the pre-existing European Economic Community. With a population of almost 500 million, the _____ generates an estimated 30% share (US$18.4 trillion in 2008) of the nominal gross world product.
   a. European Union
   b. ACCRA Cost of Living Index
   c. European Court of Justice
   d. ACEA agreement

18. _____ is a Regional Trade Agreement among Argentina, Brazil, Paraguay and Uruguay founded in 1991 by the Treaty of Asunci>ón, which was later amended and updated by the 1994 Treaty of Ouro Preto. Its purpose is to promote free trade and the fluid movement of goods, people, and currency.

   _____ origins trace back to 1985 when Presidents Ra>úl Alfons>ín of Argentina and Jos>é Sarney of Brazil signed the Argentina-Brazil Integration and Economics Cooperation Program or PICE .

   a. 100-year flood
   b. Free trade area
   c. 130-30 fund
   d. Mercosur

19. A _____ is:

- Rewrite _____, in generative grammar and computer science
- Standardization, a formal and widely-accepted statement, fact, definition, or qualification
- Operation, a determinate _____ for performing a mathematical operation and obtaining a certain result (Mathematics, Logic)
    - Unary operation
    - Binary operation
- _____ of inference, a function from sets of formulae to formulae (Mathematics, Logic)
- _____ of thumb, principle with broad application that is not intended to be strictly accurate or reliable for every situation. Also often simply referred to as a _____
- Moral, an atomic element of a moral code for guiding choices in human behavior
- Heuristic, a quantized '_____' which shows a tendency or probability for successful function
- A regulation, as in sports
- A Production _____, as in computer science
- Procedural law, a _____ set governing the application of laws to cases
    - A law, which may informally be called a '_____'
    - A court ruling, a decision by a court
- In the U.S. Government, a regulation mandated by Congress, but written or expanded upon by the Executive Branch.
- Norm (sociology), an informal but widely accepted _____, concept, truth, definition, or qualification (social norms, legal norms, coding norms)
- Norm (philosophy), a kind of sentence or a reason to act, feel or believe
- 'Rulership' is the concept of governance by a government:
    - Military _____, governance by a military body
    - Monastic _____, a collection of precepts that guides the life of monks or nuns in a religious order where the superior holds the place of Christ
- Slide _____

- '_____,' a song by Ayumi Hamasaki
- '_____,' a song by rapper Nas
- '_____s,' an album by the band The Whitest Boy Alive
- _____s: Pyaar Ka Superhit Formula, a 2003 Bollywood film
- ruler, an instrument for measuring lengths
- _____, a component of an astrolabe, circumferator or similar instrument
- The _____s, a bestselling self-help book
- _____ Project (Run Up-to-date Linux Everywhere), a project that aims to use up-to-date Linux software on old PCs
- _____ engine, a software system that helps managing business _____s
- Ja _____, a hip hop artist
    - R.U.L.E., a 2005 greatest hits album by rapper Ja _____
- '_____s,' a KMFDM song

Chapter 5. Regionalism and Multilateralism 33

   a. Rule
   b. Demand
   c. Procter ' Gamble
   d. Technocracy

20. The _____ was the outcome of the failure of negotiating governments to create the International Trade Organization (ITO.) GATT was formed in 1947 and lasted until 1994, when it was replaced by the World Trade Organization. The Bretton Woods Conference had introduced the idea for an organization to regulate trade as part of a larger plan for economic recovery after World War II.
   a. General Agreement on Trade in Services
   b. Dutch-Scandinavian Economic Pact
   c. GATT
   d. General Agreement on Tariffs and Trade

21. The _____ is a treaty of the World Trade Organization (WTO) that entered into force in January 1995 as a result of the Uruguay Round negotiations. The treaty was created to extend the multilateral trading system to service sector, in the same way the General Agreement on Tariffs and Trade (GATT) provides such a system for merchandise trade.

All members of the WTO are signatories to the GATS.

   a. General Agreement on Tariffs and Trade
   b. GATT
   c. Dutch-Scandinavian Economic Pact
   d. General Agreement on Trade in Services

22. A _____ is a duty imposed on goods when they are moved across a political boundary. They are usually associated with protectionism, the economic policy of restraining trade between nations. For political reasons, _____s are usually imposed on imported goods, although they may also be imposed on exported goods.
   a. 130-30 fund
   b. 1921 recession
   c. Tariff
   d. 100-year flood

23. The _____ is an important selective, mainly private, international organization designed by its founders to supervise and liberalize international trade. The organization officially commenced on 1 January 1995, under the Marrakesh Agreement, succeeding the 1947 General Agreement on Tariffs and Trade (GATT.)

Chapter 5. Regionalism and Multilateralism

The _____ deals with regulation of trade between participating countries; it provides a framework for negotiating and formalising trade agreements, and a dispute resolution process aimed at enforcing participants' adherence to _____ agreements which are signed by representatives of member governments and ratified by their parliaments.

   a. Backus-Kehoe-Kydland consumption correlation puzzle
   b. 2009 G-20 London summit protests
   c. Bio-energy village
   d. World Trade Organization

24. _____ is a term in international relations that refers to multiple countries working in concert on a given issue.

Most international organizations, such as the United Nations (UN) and the World Trade Organization are multilateral in nature. The main proponents of _____ have traditionally been the middle powers such as Canada, Australia and the Nordic countries.

   a. Global governance
   b. Simultaneous policy
   c. 100-year flood
   d. Multilateralism

25. _____ is exchange of capital, goods, and services across international borders or territories. In most countries, it represents a significant share of gross domestic product (GDP.) While _____ has been present throughout much of history, its economic, social, and political importance has been on the rise in recent centuries.
   a. Intra-industry trade
   b. Import license
   c. Incoterms
   d. International trade

26. The _____ of 1974 (actually enacted January 3, 1975 as Pub.L. 93-618, 88 Stat. 1978, 19 U.S.C. ch.12) was passed to help industry in the United States become more competitive or phase workers into other industries or occupations. It created fast track authority for the President to negotiate trade agreements that Congress can approve or disapprove but cannot amend or filibuster. The fast track authority created under the Act extended to 1994 and was restored in 2002 by the _____ of 2002.

a. 130-30 fund
b. Trade Act
c. 100-year flood
d. 1921 recession

Chapter 6. Balance of Payments and Foreign Exchange Markets

1. The _____ is where currency trading takes place. It is where banks and other official institutions facilitate the buying and selling of foreign currencies. FX transactions typically involve one party purchasing a quantity of one currency in exchange for paying a quantity of another.
   a. Currency swap
   b. Covered interest arbitrage
   c. Floating currency
   d. Foreign exchange market

2. _____ is a term used in accounting, economics and finance to spread the cost of an asset over the span of several years.

In simple words we can say that _____ is the reduction in the value of an asset due to usage, passage of time, wear and tear, technological outdating or obsolescence, depletion, inadequacy, rot, rust, decay or other such factors.

In accounting, _____ is a term used to describe any method of attributing the historical or purchase cost of an asset across its useful life, roughly corresponding to normal wear and tear.

   a. Net income per employee
   b. Depreciation
   c. Salvage value
   d. Historical cost

3. In economics, the _____ measures the payments that flow between any individual country and all other countries. It is used to summarize all international economic transactions for that country during a specific time period, usually a year. The _____ is determined by the country's exports and imports of goods, services, and financial capital, as well as financial transfers.
   a. Skyscraper Index
   b. Balance of payments
   c. Gross world product
   d. Gross domestic product per barrel

4. A _____ is the transfer of wealth from one party (such as a person or company) to another. A _____ is usually made in exchange for the provision of goods, services or both, or to fulfill a legal obligation.

The simplest and oldest form of _____ is barter, the exchange of one good or service for another.

a. Payment
b. Going concern
c. Soft count
d. Social gravity

5. A _____ refers to any type debt instrument, such as a loan, bond, mortgage that does not have a fixed rate of interest over the life of the instrument. Such debt typically uses an index or other base rate for establishing the interest rate for each relevant period. One of the most common rates to use as the basis for applying interest rates is the London Inter-bank Offered Rate, or LIBOR
   a. Money market
   b. Disposal tax effect
   c. Moneylender
   d. Floating interest rate

6. In economics, the _____ is one of the two primary components of the balance of payments, the other being the capital account. It is the sum of the balance of trade (exports minus imports of goods and services), net factor income (such as interest and dividends) and net transfer payments (such as foreign aid.)

$$\text{Current account} = \text{Balance of trade} \\ + \text{Net factor income from abroad} \\ + \text{Net unilateral transfers from abroad}$$

The _____ balance is one of two major metrics of the nature of a country's foreign trade (the other being the net capital outflow.)

   a. National Income and Product Accounts
   b. Compensation of employees
   c. Gross private domestic investment
   d. Current account

7. In economics, an _____ is any good or commodity, transported from one country to another country in a legitimate fashion, typically for use in trade. _____ goods or services are provided to foreign consumers by domestic producers. _____ is an important part of international trade.
   a. AD-IA Model
   b. Export
   c. ACEA agreement
   d. ACCRA Cost of Living Index

Chapter 6. Balance of Payments and Foreign Exchange Markets

8. A _____ is an object whose consumption increases the utility of the consumer, for which the quantity demanded exceeds the quantity supplied at zero price. _____s are usually modeled as having diminishing marginal utility. The first individual purchase has high utility; the second has less.
   a. Pie method
   b. Composite good
   c. Merit good
   d. Good

9. In financial accounting, the _____ is one of the accounts in shareholders' equity. Sole proprietorships have a single _____ in the owner's equity. Partnerships maintain a _____ for each of the partners.
   a. Current account
   b. Compensation of employees
   c. Capital account
   d. Net national product

10. The Organisation for Economic Co-operation and Development (_____) is an international organisation of 30 countries that accept the principles of representative democracy and free-market economy. Most _____ members are high-income economies with a high HDI and are regarded as developed countries.

    It originated in 1948 as the Organisation for European Economic Co-operation , led by Robert Marjolin of France, to help administer the Marshall Plan for the reconstruction of Europe after World War II.

    a. OECD
    b. ACCRA Cost of Living Index
    c. AD-IA Model
    d. ACEA agreement

11. _____ is the practice within the banking industry of authorizing electronic transactions done with a debit card or credit card and holding this balance as unavailable either until the merchant clears the transaction _____s can fall off the account anywhere from 1-5 days after the transaction date depending on the bank's policy; in the case of credit cards, holds may last as long as 30 days, depending on the issuing bank.

    Signature-based credit and debit card transactions are a two-step process, consisting of an authorization and a settlement.

    When a merchant swipes a customer's credit card, the credit card terminal connects to the merchant's acquirer which verifies that the customer's account is valid and that sufficient funds are available to cover the transaction's cost.

Chapter 6. Balance of Payments and Foreign Exchange Markets

a. Authorization hold
b. Issuing bank
c. Electronic funds transfer
d. Interbank network

12. In finance, the _____s between two currencies specifies how much one currency is worth in terms of the other. It is the value of a foreign natione;s currency in terms of the home natione;s currency. For example an _____ of 102 Japanese yen to the United States dollar means that JPY 102 is worth the same as USD 1.
   a. ACEA agreement
   b. Exchange rate
   c. Interbank market
   d. ACCRA Cost of Living Index

13. A _____ is the space, actual or metaphorical, in which a market operates. The term is also used in a trademark law context to denote the actual consumer environment, ie. the 'real world' in which products and services are provided and consumed.
   a. 130-30 fund
   b. 1921 recession
   c. 100-year flood
   d. Marketplace

14. _____ refers to a business or organization attempting to acquire goods or services to accomplish the goals of the enterprise. Though there are several organizations that attempt to set standards in the _____ process, processes can vary greatly between organizations. Typically the word '_____' is not used interchangeably with the word 'procurement', since procurement typically includes Expediting, Supplier Quality, and Traffic and Logistics (T'L) in addition to _____.
   a. 100-year flood
   b. Free port
   c. Purchasing
   d. 130-30 fund

15. _____ is the number of goods/services that can be purchased with a unit of currency. For example, if you had taken one dollar to a store in the 1950s, you would have been able to buy a greater number of items than you would today, indicating that you would have had a greater _____ in the 1950s. Currency can be either a commodity money, like gold or silver, or fiat currency like US dollars.

a. Human Poverty Index
b. Compliance cost
c. Genuine progress indicator
d. Purchasing power

16. The _____ theory uses the long-term equilibrium exchange rate of two currencies to equalize their purchasing power. Developed by Gustav Cassel in 1920, it is based on the law of one price: the theory states that, in ideally efficient markets, identical goods should have only one price.

This purchasing power SEM rate equalizes the purchasing power of different currencies in their home countries for a given basket of goods.

a. Measures of national income and output
b. Purchasing power parity
c. Gross national product
d. Bureau of Labor Statistics

17. _____s are cash, evidence of an ownership interest in an entity or deliver, cash or another _____.

_____s can be categorized by form depending on whether they are cash instruments or derivative instruments:

- Cash instruments are _____s whose value is determined directly by markets. They can be divided into securities, which are readily transferable, and other cash instruments such as loans and deposits, where both borrower and lender have to agree on a transfer.
- Derivative instruments are _____s which derive their value from the value and characteristics of one or more underlying assets. They can be divided into exchange-traded derivatives and over-the-counter (OTC) derivatives.

Alternatively, _____s can be categorized by 'asset class' depending on whether they are equity based (reflecting ownership of the issuing entity) or debt based (reflecting a loan the investor has made to the issuing entity.) If it is debt, it can be further categorised into short term (less than one year) or long term.

Foreign Exchange instruments and transactions are neither debt nor equity based and belong in their own category.

Chapter 6. Balance of Payments and Foreign Exchange Markets

a. Municipal Bond Arbitrage
b. Market liquidity
c. Fundamentally based indexes
d. Financial instrument

18. A _____ is a party that mediates between a buyer and a seller. A _____ who also acts as a seller or as a buyer becomes a principal party to the deal. Distinguish agent: one who acts on behalf of a principal.
    a. No call, no show
    b. Full-time
    c. Primary labor market
    d. Broker

19. _____ is money accepted for exchange of goods in an economy. The prevalence of one money over another arises, usually, when a government designates through decrees that the government shall accept only particular notes and coins in payment for taxes. Typically, money of _____ consists of stamped coins and minted paper bills.
    a. Security thread
    b. Currency
    c. Local currency
    d. Totnes pound

20. The _____ or cash market is a commodities or securities market in which goods are sold for cash and delivered immediately. Contracts bought and sold on these markets are immediately effective. _____s can operate wherever the infrastructure exists to conduct the transaction.
    a. Spot market
    b. Currency band
    c. Foreign exchange trading
    d. Triangular arbitrage

21. _____ describes a deliberate attempt to interfere with the free and fair operation of the market and create artificial, false or misleading appearances with respect to the price of a security, commodity or currency. _____ is prohibited under Section 9(a)(2) of the Securities Exchange Act of 1934, and in Australia under Section s 1041A of the Corporations Act 2001. The Act defines _____ as transactions which create an artificial price or maintain an artificial price for a tradable security.

a. Market manipulation
b. Managerial economics
c. Legal monopoly
d. Net domestic product

22. _____ in economics and business is the result of an exchange and from that trade we assign a numerical monetary value to a good, service or asset. If Alice trades Bob 4 apples for an orange, the _____ of an orange is 4 apples. Inversely, the _____ of an apple is 1/4 oranges.
   a. Price war
   b. Premium pricing
   c. Price book
   d. Price

23. _____ is the price of a commodity such as a good or service in terms of another; ie, the ratio of two prices. A _____ may be expressed in terms of a ratio between any two prices or the ratio between the price of one particular good and a weighted average of all other goods available in the market. A _____ is an opportunity cost.
   a. Relative price
   b. False shortage
   c. Food cooperative
   d. False economy

24. _____ is a broad label that refers to any individuals or households that use goods and services generated within the economy. The concept of a _____ is used in different contexts, so that the usage and significance of the term may vary.

Typically when business people and economists talk of _____s they are talking about person as _____, an aggregated commodity item with little individuality other than that expressed in the buy/not-buy decision.

   a. Consumer
   b. 130-30 fund
   c. 100-year flood
   d. 1921 recession

25. A _____ is a measure of the average price of consumer goods and services purchased by households. A _____ measures a price change for a constant market basket of goods and services from one period to the next within the same area (city, region, or nation.) It is a price index determined by measuring the price of a standard group of goods meant to represent the typical market basket of a typical urban consumer.

Chapter 6. Balance of Payments and Foreign Exchange Markets

a. CPI
b. Lipstick index
c. Cost-of-living index
d. Consumer price index

26. _____ is sometimes referred to as _____, actually it means Economic Monetary Union.

First ideas of an economic and monetary union in Europe were raised well before establishing the European Communities. For example, already in the League of Nations, Gustav Stresemann asked in 1929 for a European currency (Link) against the background of an increased economic division due to a number of new nation states in Europe after WWI.

a. European Monetary System
b. Euro Interbank Offered Rate
c. Exchange rate mechanism
d. European Monetary Union

27. An economic and _____ is a single market with a common currency. It is to be distinguished from a mere currency union, which does not involve a single market. This is the fifth stage of economic integration.
a. Free trade zone
b. Commercial invoice
c. Customs union
d. Monetary Union

28. A _____ is a normalized average (typically a weighted average) of prices for a given class of goods or services in a given region, during a given interval of time. It is a statistic designed to help to compare how these prices, taken as a whole, differ between time periods or geographical locations.

Price indices have several potential uses.

a. Two-part tariff
b. Price index
c. Transactional Net Margin Method
d. Product sabotage

Chapter 6. Balance of Payments and Foreign Exchange Markets

29. A _____, reserve bank, or monetary authority is the entity responsible for the monetary policy of a country or of a group of member states. It is a bank that can lend money to other banks in times of need. Its primary responsibility is to maintain the stability of the national currency and money supply, but more active duties include controlling subsidized-loan interest rates, and acting as a lender of last resort to the banking sector during times of financial crisis (private banks often being integral to the national financial system.)

   a. Central Bank
   b. 1921 recession
   c. 100-year flood
   d. 130-30 fund

30. The _____ is one of the world's most important central banks, responsible for monetary policy covering the 16 member States of the Eurozone. It was established by the European Union (EU) in 1998 with its headquarters in Frankfurt, Germany.

   The predecessor to the _____ was the European Monetary Institute .

   a. European Central Bank
   b. ACEA agreement
   c. ACCRA Cost of Living Index
   d. AD-IA Model

31. _____ is a form of risk that arises from the change in price of one currency against another. Whenever investors or companies have assets or business operations across national borders, they face _____ if their positions are not hedged.

   - Transaction risk is the risk that exchange rates will change unfavourably over time. It can be hedged against using forward currency contracts;
   - Translation risk is an accounting risk, proportional to the amount of assets held in foreign currencies. Changes in the exchange rate over time will render a report inaccurate, and so assets are usually balanced by borrowings in that currency.

   The exchange risk associated with a foreign denominated instrument is a key element in foreign investment. This risk flows from differential monetary policy and growth in real productivity, which results in differential inflation rates.

   a. Transaction risk
   b. Risk neutral
   c. Taleb distribution
   d. Currency risk

Chapter 6. Balance of Payments and Foreign Exchange Markets

32. _____s is the social science that studies the production, distribution, and consumption of goods and services. The term _____s comes from the Ancient Greek οἰκονομία from οἶκος (oikos, 'house') + νόμος (nomos, 'custom' or 'law'), hence 'rules of the house(hold)'. Current _____ models developed out of the broader field of political economy in the late 19th century, owing to a desire to use an empirical approach more akin to the physical sciences.
    a. Opportunity cost
    b. Inflation
    c. Energy economics
    d. Economic

33. _____s are financial contracts whose values are derived from the value of something else (known as the underlying.) The underlying value on which a _____ is based can be an asset (e.g., commodities, equities (stocks), residential mortgages, commercial real estate, loans, bonds), an index (e.g., interest rates, exchange rates, stock market indices, consumer price index (CPI) -- see inflation _____s), weather conditions bonds or other forms of credit.
    a. Second derivative
    b. 130-30 fund
    c. 100-year flood
    d. Derivative

34. _____ is a financial term which measures the proportion of money invested in the same industry sector. For example, a stock portfolio with a total worth of $500,000, with $100,000 in semiconductor industry stocks, would have a 20% exposure in 'chip' stocks.
    a. Random walk hypothesis
    b. Market exposure
    c. Martingale pricing
    d. Put-call parity

35. The _____ is a market for contracts that ensure the future delivery of a foreign currency at a specified exchange rate. The price of a forward contract is known as the forward rate.

Forward rates are usually negotiated for delivery one month, three months, or one year after the date of the contract's creation.

    a. Chained dollars
    b. Cost of delay
    c. Market moving information
    d. Forward exchange market

Chapter 6. Balance of Payments and Foreign Exchange Markets

36. A _____ is an agreement between two parties to buy or sell an asset at a specified point of time in the future. The price of the underlying instrument, in whatever form, is paid before control of the instrument changes. This is one of the many forms of buy/sell orders where the time of trade is not the time where the securities themselves are exchanged.

   a. Delta One
   b. Notional amount
   c. Risk-neutral measure
   d. Forward contract

37. The _____ is the over-the-counter financial market in contracts for future delivery, so called forward contracts. Forward contracts are personalized between parties. The _____ is a general term used to describe the informal market by which these contracts are entered into.

   a. Delta neutral
   b. Forward market
   c. Market data
   d. Convertible arbitrage

38. Economics:

   - _____ ,the desire to own something and the ability to pay for it
   - _____ curve, a graphic representation of a _____ schedule
   - _____ deposit, the money in checking accounts
   - _____ pull theory, the theory that inflation occurs when _____ for goods and services exceeds existing supplies
   - _____ schedule, a table that lists the quantity of a good a person will buy it each different price
   - _____ side economics, the school of economics at believes government spending and tax cuts open economy by raising _____

   a. Production
   b. Variability
   c. McKesson ' Robbins scandal
   d. Demand

39. The _____ is the official currency of 16 of the 27 member states of the European Union (EU.) The states, known collectively as the Eurozone, are Austria, Belgium, Cyprus, Finland, France, Germany, Greece, Ireland, Italy, Luxembourg, Malta, the Netherlands, Portugal, Slovakia, Slovenia, and Spain. The currency is also used in a further five European countries, with and without formal agreements and is consequently used daily by some 327 million Europeans.

a. Equity capital market
b. Import and Export Price Indices
c. IRS Code 3401
d. Euro

40. _____ is the a method of technical and economic research of the systems for purpose to optimize a parity between system's consumer functions or properties and expenses to achieve those functions or properties.

This methodology for continuous perfection of production, industrial technologies, organizational structures was developed by Juryj Sobolev in 1948 at the 'Perm telephone factory'

- 1948 Juryj Sobolev - the first success in application of a method analysis at the 'Perm telephone factory' .
- 1949 - the first application for the invention as result of use of the new method.

Today in economically developed countries practically each enterprise or the company use methodology of the kind of functional-cost analysis as a practice of the quality management, most full satisfying to principles of standards of series ISO 9000.

- Interest of consumer not in products itself, but the advantage which it will receive from its usage.
- The consumer aspires to reduce his expenses
- Functions needed by consumer can be executed in the various ways, and, hence, with various efficiency and expenses. Among possible alternatives of realization of functions exist such in which the parity of quality and the price is the optimal for the consumer.

The goal of _____ is achievement of the highest consumer satisfaction of production at simultaneous decrease in all kinds of industrial expenses Classical _____ has three English synonyms - Value Engineering, Value Management, Value Analysis.

a. Staple financing
b. Monopoly wage
c. Willingness to pay
d. Function cost analysis

41. The term _____, as used in currency trading, refers to the premium (or discount) resulting from a forward contract to be executed in the future at a forward rate. The premium is calculated as follows:

((forwardrate − spotrate) / spotrate) * (12 / numberofmonthsforward) * 100

The resulting value is a percentage and termed a premium if it is positive. If the resulting percentage is negative, it is a forward discount.

Chapter 6. Balance of Payments and Foreign Exchange Markets

a. Forward premium
b. Fast moving consumer goods
c. 130-30 fund
d. 100-year flood

42. Discounting is a financial mechanism in which a debtor obtains the right to delay payments to a creditor, for a defined period of time, in exchange for a charge or fee. Essentially, the party that owes money in the present purchases the right to delay the payment until some future date. The _____, or charge, is simply the difference between the original amount owed in the present and the amount that has to be paid in the future to settle the debt.
   a. Certified Risk Manager
   b. Reinsurance
   c. Discount
   d. Reliability theory

43. The _____ (often called 'the Chicago Merc,' or 'the Merc') is an American financial and commodity derivative exchange based in Chicago. The _____ was founded in 1898 as the Chicago Butter and Egg Board. Originally, the exchange was a non-profit organization.
   a. New Economic Policy
   b. Delancey Street Foundation
   c. South Sea Company
   d. Chicago Mercantile Exchange

44. A _____ is a foreign exchange agreement between two parties to exchange principal and fixed rate interest payments on a loan in one currency for principal and fixed rate interest payments on an equal (regarding net present value) loan in another currency. _____s are motivated by comparative advantage. _____s were introduced by the World Bank in 1981 to obtain Swiss franks and German marks by exchanging cash flows with IBM.
   a. Currency swap
   b. Non-deliverable forward
   c. Foreign exchange spot trading
   d. Strong dollar policy

45. A _____ is a financial contract between two parties, the buyer and the seller of this type of option. It is the option to buy shares of stock at a specified time in the future. Often it is simply labeled a 'call'. The buyer of the option has the right, but not the obligation to buy an agreed quantity of a particular commodity or financial instrument (the underlying instrument) from the seller of the option at a certain time (the expiration date) for a certain price (the strike price).

Chapter 6. Balance of Payments and Foreign Exchange Markets

a. Call option
b. Synthetic underlying position
c. Moneyness
d. Put option

46. In options, the _____ is a key variable in a derivatives contract between two parties. Where the contract requires delivery of the underlying instrument, the trade will be at the _____, regardless of the spot price (market price) of the underlying instrument at that time.

Definition - The fixed price at which the owner of an option can purchase, in the case of a call in the case of a put, the underlying security or commodity.

a. Binary option
b. Strike price
c. Married put
d. Calendar spread

47. A _____ is a financial contract between two parties, the seller (writer) and the buyer of the option. The buyer acquires a short position offering the right, but not obligation, to sell the underlying instrument at an agreed-upon price (the strike price.) If the buyer exercises the right granted by the option, the seller has the obligation to purchase the underlying at the strike price.

a. Synthetic underlying position
b. Bull spread
c. Put option
d. Bear spread

Chapter 7. Exchange-Rate Systems, Past to Present

1. The _____ is an international organization that oversees the global financial system by following the macroeconomic policies of its member countries, in particular those with an impact on exchange rates and the balance of payments. It is an organization formed to stabilize international exchange rates and facilitate development. It also offers financial and technical assistance to its members, making it an international lender of last resort.

    a. ACEA agreement
    b. ACCRA Cost of Living Index
    c. Office of Thrift Supervision
    d. International Monetary Fund

2. _____ is money declared by a government to be legal tender. The term derives from the Latin fiat, meaning 'let it be done'. _____ achieves value because a government accepts it in payment of taxes and says it can be used within the country as a 'tender' to pay all debts.

    a. World currency
    b. Fiat money
    c. Devaluation
    d. Currency board

3. The _____ of monetary management established the rules for commercial and financial relations among the world's major industrial states in the mid 20th Century. The _____ was the first example of a fully negotiated monetary order intended to govern monetary relations among independent nation-states.

    Preparing to rebuild the international economic system as World War II was still raging, 730 delegates from all 44 Allied nations gathered at the Mount Washington Hotel in Bretton Woods, New Hampshire, United States, for the United Nations Monetary and Financial Conference.

    a. 100-year flood
    b. Bretton Woods system
    c. 130-30 fund
    d. 1921 recession

4. _____ is the quality of paper money substitutes which entitles the holder to redeem them on demand into money proper.

    Historically, the banknote has followed a common or very similar pattern in the western nations. Originally decentralized and issued from various independent banks, it was gradually brought under state control and became a monopoly privilege of the central banks.

Chapter 7. Exchange-Rate Systems, Past to Present

a. Dollarization
b. Devaluation
c. Currency board
d. Convertibility

5. The _____ is a monetary system in which a region's common medium of exchange are paper notes that are normally freely convertible into pre-set, fixed quantities of gold. The _____ is not currently used by any government, having been replaced completely by fiat currency. Gold certificates were used as paper currency in the United States from 1882 to 1933, these certificates were freely convertable into gold coins.

In the 1790s Britain suffered a massive shortage of silver coinage and ceased to mint larger silver coins.

a. 100-year flood
b. 1921 recession
c. Gold standard
d. 130-30 fund

6. The _____ is an international organization of central banks which 'fosters international monetary and financial cooperation and serves as a bank for central banks.' It is not accountable to any national government. The BIS carries out its work through subcommittees, the secretariats it hosts, and through its annual General Meeting of all members. It also provides banking services, but only to central banks, or to international organizations like itself.

a. 130-30 fund
b. 1921 recession
c. 100-year flood
d. Bank for International Settlements

7. _____, 1st Baron Keynes was a renowned economist from Britain whose many ideas on economic and political theories as well as on many governments' monetary policies influenced America. He advocated a government that played an active role in the lives of people regarding business, economy, etc. In this role, the government would use fiscal measures to reduce the consequences of recessions, economic depressions and booms.

a. Adolph Fischer
b. Adolf Hitler
c. Adam Smith
d. John Maynard Keynes

Chapter 7. Exchange-Rate Systems, Past to Present

8. _____ is the practice within the banking industry of authorizing electronic transactions done with a debit card or credit card and holding this balance as unavailable either until the merchant clears the transaction _____s can fall off the account anywhere from 1-5 days after the transaction date depending on the bank's policy; in the case of credit cards, holds may last as long as 30 days, depending on the issuing bank.

Signature-based credit and debit card transactions are a two-step process, consisting of an authorization and a settlement.

When a merchant swipes a customer's credit card, the credit card terminal connects to the merchant's acquirer which verifies that the customer's account is valid and that sufficient funds are available to cover the transaction's cost.

   a. Interbank network
   b. Issuing bank
   c. Electronic funds transfer
   d. Authorization hold

9. _____s is the social science that studies the production, distribution, and consumption of goods and services. The term _____s comes from the Ancient Greek oá¼°κονομῖα from oá¼¶κος (oikos, 'house') + vÏŒμος (nomos, 'custom' or 'law'), hence 'rules of the house(hold)'. Current _____ models developed out of the broader field of political economy in the late 19th century, owing to a desire to use an empirical approach more akin to the physical sciences.
   a. Energy economics
   b. Inflation
   c. Economic
   d. Opportunity cost

10. _____ is money accepted for exchange of goods in an economy. The prevalence of one money over another arises, usually, when a government designates through decrees that the government shall accept only particular notes and coins in payment for taxes. Typically, money of _____ consists of stamped coins and minted paper bills.
   a. Local currency
   b. Totnes pound
   c. Security thread
   d. Currency

Chapter 7. Exchange-Rate Systems, Past to Present

11. Economics:

    - _____, the desire to own something and the ability to pay for it
    - _____ curve, a graphic representation of a _____ schedule
    - _____ deposit, the money in checking accounts
    - _____ pull theory, the theory that inflation occurs when _____ for goods and services exceeds existing supplies
    - _____ schedule, a table that lists the quantity of a good a person will buy it each different price
    - _____ side economics, the school of economics at believes government spending and tax cuts open economy by raising _____

    a. McKesson ' Robbins scandal
    b. Demand
    c. Production
    d. Variability

12. The United Nations Monetary and Financial Conference, commonly known as _____, was a gathering of 730 delegates from all 44 Allied nations at the Mount Washington Hotel, situated in Bretton Woods, New Hampshire to regulate the international monetary and financial order after the conclusion of World War II.

The conference was held from 1 July to 22 July 1944 in July, when the agreements were signed to set up the International Bank for Reconstruction and Development (IBRD), the General Agreement on Tariffs and Trade (GATT), and the International Monetary Fund (IMF.)

As a result of the conference, the Bretton Woods system of exchange rate management was set up, which remained in place until the early 1970s.

   a. 1921 recession
   b. 130-30 fund
   c. 100-year flood
   d. Bretton Woods Conference

13. The _____ was the outcome of the failure of negotiating governments to create the International Trade Organization (ITO.) GATT was formed in 1947 and lasted until 1994, when it was replaced by the World Trade Organization. The Bretton Woods Conference had introduced the idea for an organization to regulate trade as part of a larger plan for economic recovery after World War II.

a. General Agreement on Trade in Services
b. Dutch-Scandinavian Economic Pact
c. GATT
d. General Agreement on Tariffs and Trade

14. A _____ is a duty imposed on goods when they are moved across a political boundary. They are usually associated with protectionism, the economic policy of restraining trade between nations. For political reasons, _____s are usually imposed on imported goods, although they may also be imposed on exported goods.

   a. 130-30 fund
   b. 1921 recession
   c. 100-year flood
   d. Tariff

15. The _____ is an international financial institution that provides financial and technical assistance to developing countries for development programs (e.g. bridges, roads, schools, etc.) with the stated goal of reducing poverty.

The _____ differs from the _____ Group, in that the _____ comprises only two institutions:

- International Bank for Reconstruction and Development (IBRD)
- International Development Association (IDA)

Whereas the latter incorporates these two in addition to three more:

- International Finance Corporation (IFC)
- Multilateral Investment Guarantee Agency (MIGA)
- International Centre for Settlement of Investment Disputes (ICSID)

John Maynard Keynes (right) represented the UK at the conference, and Harry Dexter White represented the US.

The _____ is one of two major financial institutions created as a result of the Bretton Woods Conference in 1944. The International Monetary Fund, a related but separate institution, is the second.

   a. World Bank
   b. Flow to Equity-Approach
   c. Financial costs of the 2003 Iraq War
   d. Bank-State-Branch

16. _____ is a fee paid on borrowed assets. It is the price paid for the use of borrowed money , or, money earned by deposited funds . Assets that are sometimes lent with _____ include money, shares, consumer goods through hire purchase, major assets such as aircraft, and even entire factories in finance lease arrangements.
   a. Interest
   b. Internal debt
   c. Insolvency
   d. Asset protection

17. An _____ is the price a borrower pays for the use of money they do not own, for instance a small company might borrow from a bank to kick start their business, and the return a lender receives for deferring the use of funds, by lending it to the borrower. _____s are normally expressed as a percentage rate over the period of one year.

   _____s targets are also a vital tool of monetary policy and are used to control variables like investment, inflation, and unemployment.

   a. Arrow-Debreu model
   b. Enterprise value
   c. ACCRA Cost of Living Index
   d. Interest rate

18. _____ is an economic concept, expressed as a basic algebraic identity that relates interest rates and exchange rates. The identity is theoretical, and usually follows from assumptions imposed in economics models. There is evidence to support as well as to refute the concept.
   a. Interest rate parity
   b. Investment protection
   c. Ask price
   d. Asset specificity

19. The _____ was the primary plan of the United States for rebuilding and creating a stronger foundation for the countries of Western Europe, and repelling communism after World War II. The initiative was named for Secretary of State George Marshall and was largely the creation of State Department officials, especially William L. Clayton and George F. Kennan. George Marshall spoke of the administration's want to help European recovery in his address at Harvard University in June 1947.
   a. Marshall Plan
   b. 100-year flood
   c. 1921 recession
   d. 130-30 fund

20. A _____ is a currency which is held in significant quantities by many governments and institutions as part of their foreign exchange reserves. It also tends to be the international pricing currency for products traded on a global market, such as oil, gold, etc.

This permits the issuing country to purchase the commodities at a marginally cheaper rate than other nations, which must exchange their currency with each purchase and pay a transaction cost.

a. Texas redbacks
b. World currency
c. Reserve currency
d. Currency board

21. The _____ was the first attempt at European monetary cooperation in the 1970s, aiming at limiting fluctuations between different European currencies. It was an attempt at creating a single currency band for the European Economic Community (EEC), essentially pegging all the EEC currencies to one another.

Pierre Werner presented a report on economic and monetary union to the EEC on 8 October 1970.

a. 1921 recession
b. Snake in the tunnel
c. 100-year flood
d. 130-30 fund

22. The _____ was a December 1971 agreement that ended the fixed exchange rates established at the Bretton Woods Conference of 1944.

The Bretton Woods Conference of 1944 established an international fixed exchange rate regime in which currencies were pegged to the United States dollar, which was based on the gold standard.

By 1970, however, it was clear that the exchange rate regime was under threat, as the United States dollar was greatly overvalued because of heavy American spending on Lyndon B. Johnson's Great Society and the Vietnam War.

a. Hanseatic League
b. History of capitalism
c. Commercial Revolution
d. Smithsonian agreement

Chapter 7. Exchange-Rate Systems, Past to Present

23. _____ is a term in economics, where demand for one good or service occurs as a result of demand for another. This may occur as the former is a part of production of the second. For example, demand for coal leads to _____ for mining, as coal must be mined for coal to be consumed.
    a. Days Sales Outstanding
    b. Rate risk
    c. Derived demand
    d. Leontief production function

24. _____ was an American economist, statistician and public intellectual, and a recipient of the Nobel Memorial Prize in Economic Sciences. He is best known among scholars for his theoretical and empirical research, especially consumption analysis, monetary history and theory, and for his demonstration of the complexity of stabilization policy. A global public followed his restatement of a political philosophy that insisted on minimizing the role of government in favor of the private sector.
    a. Adolph Fischer
    b. Milton Friedman
    c. Adam Smith
    d. Adolf Hitler

25. The _____ was signed by the then G6 on February 22, 1987 in Paris, France. Italy had been an invited member, but declined to finalize the agreement. The goal of the _____ was to stabilize the international currency markets and halt the continued decline of the US Dollar caused by the Plaza Accord .
    a. 100-year flood
    b. Plaza Agreement
    c. Mellonomics
    d. Louvre Accord

26. In international commerce and politics, an _____ is the prohibition of commerce (division of trade) and trade with a certain country, in order to isolate it and to put its government into a difficult internal situation, given that the effects of the _____ are often able to make its economy suffer from the initiative.

The _____ is usually used as a political punishment for some previous disagreed policies or acts, but its economic nature frequently raises doubts about the real interests that the prohibition serves.

One of the most comprehensive attempts at an _____ happened during the Napoleonic Wars.

Chapter 7. Exchange-Rate Systems, Past to Present

a. Embargo
b. Optimum currency area
c. International finance
d. Overshooting model

27. The Plaza Accord or _____ was an agreement between the governments of France, West Germany, Japan, the United States and the United Kingdom, agreeing to depreciate the US dollar in relation to the Japanese yen and German Deutsche Mark by intervening in currency markets. The five governments signed the accord on September 22, 1985 at the Plaza Hotel in New York City.

The exchange rate value of the dollar versus the yen declined by 51% from 1985 to 1987.

a. Mellonomics
b. 100-year flood
c. Plaza Agreement
d. Louvre Accord

28. In finance, the _____s between two currencies specifies how much one currency is worth in terms of the other. It is the value of a foreign natione;s currency in terms of the home natione;s currency. For example an _____ of 102 Japanese yen to the United States dollar means that JPY 102 is worth the same as USD 1.

a. ACCRA Cost of Living Index
b. Interbank market
c. ACEA agreement
d. Exchange rate

29. In cases of extreme appreciation or depreciation, a central bank will normally intervene to stabilize the currency. Thus, the exchange rate regimes of floating currencies may more technically be known as a _____. A central bank might, for instance, allow a currency price to float freely between an upper and lower bound, a price 'ceiling' and 'floor'.

a. Continuous linked settlement
b. Triangular arbitrage
c. Managed float
d. Foreign exchange reserves

30. A consumer price index (_____) is a measure of the average price of consumer goods and services purchased by households. A consumer price index measures a price change for a constant market basket of goods and services from one period to the next within the same area (city, region, or nation.) It is a price index determined by measuring the price of a standard group of goods meant to represent the typical market basket of a typical urban consumer.

Chapter 7. Exchange-Rate Systems, Past to Present

a. Hedonic price index
b. Cost-of-living index
c. Lipstick index
d. CPI

31. The _____ is where currency trading takes place. It is where banks and other official institutions facilitate the buying and selling of foreign currencies. FX transactions typically involve one party purchasing a quantity of one currency in exchange for paying a quantity of another.
   a. Foreign exchange market
   b. Currency swap
   c. Covered interest arbitrage
   d. Floating currency

32. A _____ is a monetary authority which is required to maintain a fixed exchange rate with a foreign currency. This policy objective requires the conventional objectives of a central bank to be subordinated to the exchange rate target.

The main qualities of an orthodox _____ are:

- A _____'s foreign currency reserves must be sufficient to ensure that all holders of its notes and coins (and all banks creditor of a Reserve Account at the _____) can convert them into the reserve currency (usually 110-115% of the monetary base M0.)
- A _____ maintains absolute, unlimited convertibility between its notes and coins and the currency against which they are pegged (the anchor currency), at a fixed rate of exchange, with no restrictions on current-account or capital-account transactions.
- A _____ only earns profit from interests on foreign reserves (less the expense of note-issuing), and does not engage in forward-exchange transactions. These foreign reserves exist (1) because local notes have been issued in exchange, or (2) because commercial banks must by regulation deposit a minimum reserve at the _____. (1) generates a seignorage revenue. (2) is the revenue on minimum reserves (revenue of investment activities less cost of minimum reserves remuneration)
- A _____ has no discretionary powers to effect monetary policy and does not lend to the government. Governments cannot print money, and can only tax or borrow to meet their spending commitments.
- A _____ does not act as a lender of last resort to commercial banks, and does not regulate reserve requirements.
- A _____ does not attempt to manipulate interest rates by establishing a discount rate like a central bank. The peg with the foreign currency tends to keep interest rates and inflation very closely aligned to those in the country against whose currency the peg is fixed.

The _____ in question will no longer issue fiat money but instead will only issue one unit of local currency for each unit (or decided amount) of foreign currency it has in its vault (often a hard currency such as the U.S. dollar or the euro.) The surplus on the balance of payments of that country is reflected by higher deposits local banks hold at the central bank as well as (initially) higher deposits of the (net) exporting firms at their local banks.

a. Currency competition
b. Currency board
c. Reserve currency
d. Petrodollar

33. The _____ is a trilateral trade bloc in North America created by the governments of the United States, Canada, and Mexico. The agreement creating the trade bloc came into force on January 1, 1994. It superseded the Canada-United States Free Trade Agreement between the U.S. and Canada.
   a. North American Free Trade Agreement
   b. Federal Reserve Bank Notes
   c. Case-Shiller Home Price Indices
   d. Demand-side technologies

34. _____ occurs when the inhabitants of a country use foreign currency in parallel to or instead of the domestic currency.

_____ can occur

- unofficially, when private agents prefer the foreign currency over the domestic currency. They hold for example deposits in the foreign currency because of a bad track record of the local currency.

- semiofficially (or officially bimonetary systems), where foreign currency is legal tender, but plays a secondary role to domestic currency

- officially, when a country ceases to issue the domestic currency and uses only foreign currency. It adopts the foreign currency as legal tender.

The term _____ is not only applied to usage of the United States dollar, but also generally to the use of any foreign currency as the national currency.

   a. Currency board
   b. Dollarization
   c. Commodity money
   d. World currency

35. A _____ or a flexible exchange rate is a type of exchange rate regime wherein a currency's value is allowed to fluctuate according to the foreign exchange market. A currency that uses a _____ is known as a floating currency. The opposite of a _____ is a fixed exchange rate.

a. Floating currency
b. Foreign exchange market
c. Trade Weighted US dollar Index
d. Floating exchange rate

Chapter 8. The Power of Arbitrage—Purchasing Power and Interest Rate Parities

1. A _____, reserve bank, or monetary authority is the entity responsible for the monetary policy of a country or of a group of member states. It is a bank that can lend money to other banks in times of need. Its primary responsibility is to maintain the stability of the national currency and money supply, but more active duties include controlling subsidized-loan interest rates, and acting as a lender of last resort to the banking sector during times of financial crisis (private banks often being integral to the national financial system.)
    a. 130-30 fund
    b. 1921 recession
    c. 100-year flood
    d. Central Bank

2. The _____ is one of the world's most important central banks, responsible for monetary policy covering the 16 member States of the Eurozone. It was established by the European Union (EU) in 1998 with its headquarters in Frankfurt, Germany.

    The predecessor to the _____ was the European Monetary Institute .

    a. AD-IA Model
    b. ACCRA Cost of Living Index
    c. ACEA agreement
    d. European Central Bank

3. _____ is sometimes referred to as _____, actually it means Economic Monetary Union.

    First ideas of an economic and monetary union in Europe were raised well before establishing the European Communities. For example, already in the League of Nations, Gustav Stresemann asked in 1929 for a European currency (Link) against the background of an increased economic division due to a number of new nation states in Europe after WWI.

    a. Euro Interbank Offered Rate
    b. Exchange rate mechanism
    c. European Monetary System
    d. European Monetary Union

4. An economic and _____ is a single market with a common currency. It is to be distinguished from a mere currency union , which does not involve a single market. This is the fifth stage of economic integration.
    a. Commercial invoice
    b. Free trade zone
    c. Customs union
    d. Monetary Union

Chapter 8. The Power of Arbitrage—Purchasing Power and Interest Rate Parities

5. _____ is a forum for 21 Pacific Rim countries (styled 'member economies') to cooperate on regional trade and investment liberalisation and facilitation. APEC's objective is to enhance economic growth and prosperity in the region and to strengthen the Asia-Pacific community. Members account for approximately 40% of the world's population, approximately 54% of world GDP and about 44% of world trade.
   a. AD-IA Model
   b. ACCRA Cost of Living Index
   c. ACEA agreement
   d. Asia-Pacific Economic Cooperation

6. The _____ is an economic law stated as: 'In an efficient market all identical goods must have only one price.' The _____ relates to the outcome of free trade and globalization. It is the theory that some day all areas of the world will make the same amount of money as every other part of the world for equal work/product quality.

   The intuition for this law is that all sellers will flock to the highest prevailing price, and all buyers to the lowest current market price.

   a. Loss of use
   b. Precaria
   c. Leave of absence
   d. Law of one price

7. _____ refers to a business or organization attempting to acquire goods or services to accomplish the goals of the enterprise. Though there are several organizations that attempt to set standards in the _____ process, processes can vary greatly between organizations. Typically the word '_____' is not used interchangeably with the word 'procurement', since procurement typically includes Expediting, Supplier Quality, and Traffic and Logistics (T'L) in addition to _____.
   a. 130-30 fund
   b. 100-year flood
   c. Free port
   d. Purchasing

8. _____ is the number of goods/services that can be purchased with a unit of currency. For example, if you had taken one dollar to a store in the 1950s, you would have been able to buy a greater number of items than you would today, indicating that you would have had a greater _____ in the 1950s. Currency can be either a commodity money, like gold or silver, or fiat currency like US dollars.
   a. Human Poverty Index
   b. Compliance cost
   c. Genuine progress indicator
   d. Purchasing power

Chapter 8. The Power of Arbitrage—Purchasing Power and Interest Rate Parities

9. The _____ theory uses the long-term equilibrium exchange rate of two currencies to equalize their purchasing power. Developed by Gustav Cassel in 1920, it is based on the law of one price: the theory states that, in ideally efficient markets, identical goods should have only one price.

This purchasing power SEM rate equalizes the purchasing power of different currencies in their home countries for a given basket of goods.

   a. Bureau of Labor Statistics
   b. Measures of national income and output
   c. Gross national product
   d. Purchasing power parity

10. _____ in economics and business is the result of an exchange and from that trade we assign a numerical monetary value to a good, service or asset. If Alice trades Bob 4 apples for an orange, the _____ of an orange is 4 apples. Inversely, the _____ of an apple is 1/4 oranges.

   a. Price book
   b. Price war
   c. Premium pricing
   d. Price

11. In finance, the _____s between two currencies specifies how much one currency is worth in terms of the other. It is the value of a foreign natione;s currency in terms of the home natione;s currency. For example an _____ of 102 Japanese yen to the United States dollar means that JPY 102 is worth the same as USD 1.

   a. ACCRA Cost of Living Index
   b. Interbank market
   c. ACEA agreement
   d. Exchange rate

12. A _____ is the transfer of wealth from one party (such as a person or company) to another. A _____ is usually made in exchange for the provision of goods, services or both, or to fulfill a legal obligation.

The simplest and oldest form of _____ is barter, the exchange of one good or service for another.

   a. Going concern
   b. Payment
   c. Social gravity
   d. Soft count

Chapter 8. The Power of Arbitrage—Purchasing Power and Interest Rate Parities

13. The _____ is published by The Economist as an informal way of measuring the purchasing power parity (PPP) between two currencies and provides a test of the extent to which market exchange rates result in goods costing the same in different countries. It 'seeks to make exchange-rate theory a bit more digestible'.

The index takes its name from the Big Mac, a hamburger sold at McDonald's restaurants.

a. Deindexation
b. Cost-weighted activity index
c. Rank mobility index
d. Big Mac Index

14. In economics, an _____ is any good or commodity, transported from one country to another country in a legitimate fashion, typically for use in trade. _____ goods or services are provided to foreign consumers by domestic producers. _____ is an important part of international trade.

a. AD-IA Model
b. Export
c. ACEA agreement
d. ACCRA Cost of Living Index

15. In algebra, a _____ is a function depending on n that associates a scalar, det(A), to an n×n square matrix A. The fundamental geometric meaning of a _____ is a scale factor for measure when A is regarded as a linear transformation. _____s are important both in calculus, where they enter the substitution rule for several variables, and in multilinear algebra.

For a fixed nonnegative integer n, there is a unique _____ function for the n×n matrices over any commutative ring R. In particular, this function exists when R is the field of real or complex numbers.

a. 1921 recession
b. Determinant
c. 100-year flood
d. 130-30 fund

16. In economic models, the _____ time frame assumes no fixed factors of production. Firms can enter or leave the marketplace, and the cost (and availability) of land, labor, raw materials, and capital goods can be assumed to vary. In contrast, in the short-run time frame, certain factors are assumed to be fixed, because there is not sufficient time for them to change.

a. Long-run
b. Diseconomies of scale
c. Price/performance ratio
d. Productivity world

17. The _____ is a market for contracts that ensure the future delivery of a foreign currency at a specified exchange rate. The price of a forward contract is known as the forward rate.

Forward rates are usually negotiated for delivery one month, three months, or one year after the date of the contract's creation.

a. Cost of delay
b. Forward exchange market
c. Market moving information
d. Chained dollars

18. _____ is a fee paid on borrowed assets. It is the price paid for the use of borrowed money, or, money earned by deposited funds. Assets that are sometimes lent with _____ include money, shares, consumer goods through hire purchase, major assets such as aircraft, and even entire factories in finance lease arrangements.

a. Internal debt
b. Insolvency
c. Asset protection
d. Interest

19. An _____ is the price a borrower pays for the use of money they do not own, for instance a small company might borrow from a bank to kick start their business, and the return a lender receives for deferring the use of funds, by lending it to the borrower. _____s are normally expressed as a percentage rate over the period of one year.

_____s targets are also a vital tool of monetary policy and are used to control variables like investment, inflation, and unemployment.

a. Enterprise value
b. Arrow-Debreu model
c. ACCRA Cost of Living Index
d. Interest rate

Chapter 8. The Power of Arbitrage—Purchasing Power and Interest Rate Parities

20. _____ is an economic concept, expressed as a basic algebraic identity that relates interest rates and exchange rates. The identity is theoretical, and usually follows from assumptions imposed in economics models. There is evidence to support as well as to refute the concept.
    a. Asset specificity
    b. Ask price
    c. Interest rate parity
    d. Investment protection

21. _____ is a form of arbitrage where funds are transferred abroad to take advantage of higher interest in foreign monetary centers. It involves the conversion of the domestic currency to the foreign currency to make investment; and subsequent re-conversion of the fund from the foreign currency to the domestic currency at the time of maturity. A foreign exchange risk is involved due to the possible depreciation of the foreign currency during the period of the investment.
    a. ACEA agreement
    b. AD-IA Model
    c. ACCRA Cost of Living Index
    d. Uncovered interest arbitrage

22. In economics and finance, _____ is the practice of taking advantage of a price differential between two or more markets: striking a combination of matching deals that capitalize upon the imbalance, the profit being the difference between the market prices. When used by academics, an _____ is a transaction that involves no negative cash flow at any probabilistic or temporal state and a positive cash flow in at least one state; in simple terms, a risk-free profit. A person who engages in _____ is called an arbitrageur--such as a bank or brokerage firm.
    a. Electronic trading
    b. Options Price Reporting Authority
    c. Arbitrage
    d. Alternext

23. The _____ is where currency trading takes place. It is where banks and other official institutions facilitate the buying and selling of foreign currencies. FX transactions typically involve one party purchasing a quantity of one currency in exchange for paying a quantity of another.
    a. Covered interest arbitrage
    b. Currency swap
    c. Floating currency
    d. Foreign exchange market

24. In economics, _____ means that people form their expectations about what will happen in the future based on what has happened in the past. For example, if inflation has been higher than expected in the past, people would revise expectations for the future.

One simple version of _____ is stated in the following equation, where p^e is the next year's rate of inflation that is currently expected; p^e_{-1} is this year's rate of inflation that was expected last year; and p is this year's actual rate of inflation:

$$p^e = p^e_{-1} + \lambda(p_{-1} - p^e_{-1})$$

With λ is between 0 and 1, this says that current expectations of future inflation reflect past expectations and an 'error-adjustment' term, in which current expectations are raised (or lowered) according to the gap between actual inflation and previous expectations.

a. Economic interdependence
b. Investment-specific technological progress
c. AD-IA Model
d. Adaptive expectations

25. _____ is an assumption used in many contemporary macroeconomic models, and also in other areas of contemporary economics and game theory and in other applications of rational choice theory.

Since most macroeconomic models today study decisions over many periods, the expectations of workers, consumers, and firms about future economic conditions are an essential part of the model. How to model these expectations has long been controversial, and it is well known that the macroeconomic predictions of the model may differ depending on the assumptions made about expectations

a. Balanced-growth equilibrium
b. Potential output
c. Rational expectations
d. Minimum wage

Chapter 8. The Power of Arbitrage—Purchasing Power and Interest Rate Parities

26. A _____ is a general term that describes any government policy or regulation that restricts international trade. The barriers can take many forms, including the following terms that include many restrictions in international trade within multiple countries that import and export any items of trade.

- Import duty
- Import licenses
- Export licenses
- Import quotas
- Tariffs
- Subsidies
- Non-tariff barriers to trade
- Voluntary Export Restraints
- Local Content Requirements
- Embargo

Most _____s work on the same principle: the imposition of some sort of cost on trade that raises the price of the traded products. If two or more nations repeatedly use _____s against each other, then a trade war results.

a. National Foreign Trade Council
b. Global financial system
c. Certificate of origin
d. Trade barrier

27. In finance and economics _____ or nominal rate of interest refers to the rate of interest before adjustment for inflation (in contrast with the real interest rate); or, for interest rates 'as stated' without adjustment for the full effect of compounding (also referred to as the nominal annual rate.) An interest rate is called nominal if the frequency of compounding (e.g. a month) is not identical to the basic time unit (normally a year.)

The real interest rate includes compensation for the lender's lost value due to inflation, whereas the _____ excludes inflation.

a. Risk-free interest rate
b. London Interbank Offered Rate
c. Fixed interest
d. Nominal interest rate

28. The '_____' is approximately the nominal interest rate minus the inflation rate Since the inflation rate over the course of a loan is not known initially, volatility in inflation represents a risk to both the lender and the borrower.

In economics and finance, an individual who lends money for repayment at a later point in time expects to be compensated for the time value of money, or not having the use of that money while it is lent.

a. Core inflation
b. Reflation
c. Real interest rate
d. Cost-push inflation

29. The Organisation for Economic Co-operation and Development (_____) is an international organisation of 30 countries that accept the principles of representative democracy and free-market economy. Most _____ members are high-income economies with a high HDI and are regarded as developed countries.

It originated in 1948 as the Organisation for European Economic Co-operation , led by Robert Marjolin of France, to help administer the Marshall Plan for the reconstruction of Europe after World War II.

a. OECD
b. AD-IA Model
c. ACEA agreement
d. ACCRA Cost of Living Index

Chapter 9. Global Money and Banking—Where Central Banks Fit into the World Economy

1. The _____ is the central bank of the United Kingdom and is the model on which most modern, large central banks have been based. Since 1946 it has been a state-owned institution. It was established in 1694 to act as the English Government's banker, and to this day it still acts as the banker for the UK Government.
    a. 100-year flood
    b. 1921 recession
    c. 130-30 fund
    d. Bank of England

2. A _____, reserve bank, or monetary authority is the entity responsible for the monetary policy of a country or of a group of member states. It is a bank that can lend money to other banks in times of need. Its primary responsibility is to maintain the stability of the national currency and money supply, but more active duties include controlling subsidized-loan interest rates, and acting as a lender of last resort to the banking sector during times of financial crisis (private banks often being integral to the national financial system.)
    a. 130-30 fund
    b. Central bank
    c. 1921 recession
    d. 100-year flood

3. _____ is that which is owed; usually referencing assets owed, but the term can also cover moral obligations and other interactions not requiring money. In the case of assets, _____ is a means of using future purchasing power in the present before a summation has been earned. Some companies and corporations use _____ as a part of their overall corporate finance strategy.
    a. Hard money loan
    b. Debenture
    c. Collateral Management
    d. Debt

4. _____ is the central bank of Sweden and the world's oldest central bank. It is sometimes called the Swedish National Bank or the Bank of Sweden

The Riksbank began its operations in 1668, its antecedent being Stockholms Banco (also known as the Bank of Palmstruch), which was founded by Johan Palmstruch in 1656. Although the bank was private, it was the King who chose its management: in a letter to Palmstruch he gave permission to its operations according to stated regulations.

    a. 1921 recession
    b. 130-30 fund
    c. 100-year flood
    d. Sveriges Riksbank

Chapter 9. Global Money and Banking—Where Central Banks Fit into the World

Economy

5. The term _____ refers to government debt, expenditures and revenues, or to finance (particularly financial revenue) in general.

   - _____ deficit is the budget deficit of federal or local government
   - _____ policy is the discretionary spending of governments. Contrasts with monetary policy.
   - _____ year and _____ quarter are reporting periods for firms and other agencies.

   a. Drawdown
   b. Bucket shop
   c. Fiscal
   d. Procter ' Gamble

6. A _____ is an institution willing to extend credit when no one else will.

Originally the term referred to a reserve financial institution that secured other banks or eligible institutions, as a last resort; most often the central bank of a country. The purpose of this loan and lender is to prevent the collapse of institutions that are experiencing financial difficulty, most often near collapse.

   a. Transactional account
   b. Capital requirement
   c. Time deposit
   d. Lender of last resort

7. In business and accounting, _____ are everything of value that is owned by a person or company. It is a claim on the property your income of a borrower. The balance sheet of a firm records the monetary value of the _____ owned by the firm.

   a. Amortization schedule
   b. ACCRA Cost of Living Index
   c. ACEA agreement
   d. Assets

8. _____ is the process by which the government, central bank (ii) availability of money, and (iii) cost of money or rate of interest, in order to attain a set of objectives oriented towards the growth and stability of the economy. Monetary theory provides insight into how to craft optimal _____.

_____ is referred to as either being an expansionary policy where an expansionary policy increases the total supply of money in the economy, and a contractionary policy decreases the total money supply.

Chapter 9. Global Money and Banking—Where Central Banks Fit into the World Economy

a. 130-30 fund
b. 1921 recession
c. 100-year flood
d. Monetary policy

9. In financial accounting, a _____ or statement of financial position is a summary of a person's or organization's balances. Assets, liabilities and ownership equity are listed as of a specific date, such as the end of its financial year. A _____ is often described as a snapshot of a company's financial condition.

a. Balance sheet
b. 130-30 fund
c. 100-year flood
d. 1921 recession

10. The _____ is one of the world's most important central banks, responsible for monetary policy covering the 16 member States of the Eurozone. It was established by the European Union (EU) in 1998 with its headquarters in Frankfurt, Germany.

The predecessor to the _____ was the European Monetary Institute .

a. ACCRA Cost of Living Index
b. European Central Bank
c. AD-IA Model
d. ACEA agreement

11. The accounting equation relates assets, _____, and owner's equity:

   Assets = _____ + Owner's Equity

The accounting equation is the mathematical structure of the balance sheet.

The Australian Accounting Research Foundation defines _____ as: 'future sacrifice of economic benefits that the entity is presently obliged to make to other entities as a result of past transactions and other past events.'

Probably the most accepted accounting definition of liability is the one used by the International Accounting Standards Board (IASB.) The following is a quotation from IFRS Framework:

A liability is a present obligation of the enterprise arising from past events, the settlement of which is expected to result in an outflow from the enterprise of resources embodying economic benefits

Regulations as to the recognition of _____ are different all over the world, but are roughly similar to those of the IASB.

a. Community property
b. Liabilities
c. Coase theorem
d. Competition law theory

12. _____ is money accepted for exchange of goods in an economy. The prevalence of one money over another arises, usually, when a government designates through decrees that the government shall accept only particular notes and coins in payment for taxes. Typically, money of _____ consists of stamped coins and minted paper bills.

a. Security thread
b. Local currency
c. Totnes pound
d. Currency

13. A _____ in general is a certificate of ownership that gold owners hold instead of storing the actual gold. It has both a historic meaning as a US paper currency (1882-1933) and a current meaning as a way to invest in gold. A picture of a _____ Series 1934 $100 _____, Obverse $100,000 _____, Obverse

The _____ was used from 1882 to 1933 in the United States as a form of paper currency.

a. 130-30 fund
b. 100-year flood
c. 1921 recession
d. Gold certificate

14. _____ are potential claims on the freely usable currencies of International Monetary Fund members. _____s have the ISO 4217 currency code XDR.

_____s are defined in terms of a basket of major currencies used in international trade and finance.

a. Special Drawing Rights
b. Quota share
c. Metzler paradox
d. Bilateral Investment Treaty

15. A _____ refers to any type debt instrument, such as a loan, bond, mortgage that does not have a fixed rate of interest over the life of the instrument. Such debt typically uses an index or other base rate for establishing the interest rate for each relevant period. One of the most common rates to use as the basis for applying interest rates is the London Inter-bank Offered Rate, or LIBOR
   a. Floating interest rate
   b. Moneylender
   c. Disposal tax effect
   d. Money market

16. _____ is a macroeconomic term referring to the monetary base -- that is, to highly liquid money and includes currency and vault cash. In the United States, with the beginning of the Federal Reserve System in 1913, _____ also includes deposit liabilities of the Federal Reserve System to banks.

The monetary base is typically controlled by the institution in a country that controls monetary policy.

   a. Hodrick-Prescott filter
   b. Complex multiplier
   c. Rational expectations
   d. High-powered money

17. A _____ is an intermediary used in trade to avoid the inconveniences of a pure barter system.

By contrast, as William Stanley Jevons argued, in a barter system there must be a coincidence of wants before two people can trade - one must want exactly what the other has to offer, when and where it is offered, so that the exchange can occur. A _____ permits the value of goods to be assessed and rendered in terms of the intermediary, most often, a form of money widely accepted to buy any other good.

   a. Price revolution
   b. Medium of exchange
   c. Labour economics
   d. Consumer theory

Chapter 9. Global Money and Banking—Where Central Banks Fit into the World

18. In economics, the _____ is a term relating to the money supply, the amount of money in the economy. The _____ comprises only coins, paper money, and commercial banks' reserves with the central bank. Broader measures of the money supply include the public's bank deposits.
    a. Chartalism
    b. Monetary economy
    c. Quantum economics
    d. Monetary base

19. A _____ is the accepted way, in a given market, to settle a debt. For example, while the gold standard reigned, gold or any currency convertible to gold at a fixed rate constituted such a standard. As of 2003, the US dollar and the euro are the most generally accepted standards for international settlements.
    a. Spot-future parity
    b. CFA Institute
    c. Consignment stock
    d. Standard of deferred payment

20. To act as a _____, a commodity, a form of money stored, and retrieved - and be predictably useful when it is so retrieved.

This is distinct from the standard of deferred payment function which requires acceptability to parties one owes a debt to and a minimum of opportunity to cheat others.

    a. Fiat money
    b. World currency
    c. Store of value
    d. Petrodollar

21. A _____ is a standard monetary unit of measurement of the market value/cost of goods, services, or assets. It is one of three well-known functions of money. It lends meaning to profits, losses, liability, or assets.
    a. Unit of account
    b. ACCRA Cost of Living Index
    c. ACEA agreement
    d. AD-IA Model

22. A _____ is the transfer of wealth from one party (such as a person or company) to another. A _____ is usually made in exchange for the provision of goods, services or both, or to fulfill a legal obligation.

The simplest and oldest form of _____ is barter, the exchange of one good or service for another.

a. Going concern
b. Social gravity
c. Soft count
d. Payment

23. _____ is the a method of technical and economic research of the systems for purpose to optimize a parity between system's consumer functions or properties and expenses to achieve those functions or properties.

This methodology for continuous perfection of production, industrial technologies, organizational structures was developed by Juryj Sobolev in 1948 at the 'Perm telephone factory'

- 1948 Juryj Sobolev - the first success in application of a method analysis at the 'Perm telephone factory' .
- 1949 - the first application for the invention as result of use of the new method.

Today in economically developed countries practically each enterprise or the company use methodology of the kind of functional-cost analysis as a practice of the quality management, most full satisfying to principles of standards of series ISO 9000.

- Interest of consumer not in products itself, but the advantage which it will receive from its usage.
- The consumer aspires to reduce his expenses
- Functions needed by consumer can be executed in the various ways, and, hence, with various efficiency and expenses. Among possible alternatives of realization of functions exist such in which the parity of quality and the price is the optimal for the consumer.

The goal of _____ is achievement of the highest consumer satisfaction of production at simultaneous decrease in all kinds of industrial expenses Classical _____ has three English synonyms - Value Engineering, Value Management, Value Analysis.

a. Monopoly wage
b. Function cost analysis
c. Willingness to pay
d. Staple financing

24. _____ in its classic form is defined as a company from one country making a physical investment into building a factory in another country. It is the establishment of an enterprise by a foreigner. Its definition can be extended to include investments made to acquire lasting interest in enterprises operating outside of the economy of the investor.

Chapter 9. Global Money and Banking—Where Central Banks Fit into the World Economy

a. Financial Stability Forum
b. Foreign direct investment
c. Federal Deposit Insurance Corporation
d. Non-governmental organization

25. In the United States, _____ are overnight borrowings by banks to maintain their bank reserves at the Federal Reserve. Banks keep reserves at Federal Reserve Banks to meet their reserve requirements and to clear financial transactions. Transactions in the _____ market enable depository institutions with reserve balances in excess of reserve requirements to lend reserves to institutions with reserve deficiencies.
   a. Federal funds rate
   b. Federal funds
   c. Term auction facility
   d. Federal Reserve Transparency Act

26. In the United States, the _____ is the interest rate at which private depository institutions (mostly banks) lend balances (federal funds) at the Federal Reserve to other depository institutions, usually overnight. It is the interest rate banks charge each other for loans. Changing the target rate is one way the Chairman of the Federal Reserve can influence the supply of money in the U.S. economy..
   a. Federal banking
   b. Monetary Policy Report to the Congress
   c. Federal funds rate
   d. Term auction facility

27. _____ is a fee paid on borrowed assets. It is the price paid for the use of borrowed money , or, money earned by deposited funds . Assets that are sometimes lent with _____ include money, shares, consumer goods through hire purchase, major assets such as aircraft, and even entire factories in finance lease arrangements.
   a. Asset protection
   b. Insolvency
   c. Internal debt
   d. Interest

28. An _____ is the price a borrower pays for the use of money they do not own, for instance a small company might borrow from a bank to kick start their business, and the return a lender receives for deferring the use of funds, by lending it to the borrower. _____s are normally expressed as a percentage rate over the period of one year.

_____s targets are also a vital tool of monetary policy and are used to control variables like investment, inflation, and unemployment.

a. Interest rate
b. Enterprise value
c. ACCRA Cost of Living Index
d. Arrow-Debreu model

29. _____ is sometimes referred to as _____, actually it means Economic Monetary Union.

First ideas of an economic and monetary union in Europe were raised well before establishing the European Communities. For example, already in the League of Nations, Gustav Stresemann asked in 1929 for a European currency (Link) against the background of an increased economic division due to a number of new nation states in Europe after WWI.

a. European Monetary System
b. Exchange rate mechanism
c. Euro Interbank Offered Rate
d. European Monetary Union

30. The _____ , a component of the Federal Reserve System, is charged under United States law with overseeing the nation's open market operations. It is the Federal Reserve Committee that makes key decisions about interest rates and the growth jam of the United States money supply. It is the principal organ of United States national monetary policy.

a. Fed Funds Probability
b. Federal Reserve Transparency Act
c. Primary Dealer Credit Facility
d. Federal Open Market Committee

31. An economic and _____ is a single market with a common currency. It is to be distinguished from a mere currency union , which does not involve a single market. This is the fifth stage of economic integration.

a. Commercial invoice
b. Customs union
c. Monetary Union
d. Free trade zone

32. The Organization of the Petroleum Exporting Countries is a cartel of twelve countries made up of Algeria, Angola, Ecuador, Iran, Iraq, Kuwait, Libya, Nigeria, Qatar, Saudi Arabia, the United Arab Emirates, and Venezuela. The cartel has maintained its headquarters in Vienna since 1965, and hosts regular meetings among the oil ministers of its Member Countries. Indonesia withdrew its membership in _____ in 2008 after it became a net importer of oil, but stated it would likely return if it became a net exporter in the world.

a. ACCRA Cost of Living Index
b. ACEA agreement
c. AD-IA Model
d. OPEC

33. In economics, the _____ is the term used to refer to the environment in which bonds are bought and sold between a central bank ' its regulated banks. It is not a free market process.

- To intervene in the 'business cycle', a central bank may choose to go into the _____ and buy or sell government bonds, which is known as _____ operations to increase reserves.

a. ACCRA Cost of Living Index
b. Inside money
c. Outside money
d. Open Market

34. The _____ is a bank regulation that sets the minimum reserves each bank must hold to customer deposits and notes. It would normally be in the form of fiat currency stored in a bank vault (vault cash), or with a central bank.

The reserve ratio is sometimes used as a tool in the monetary policy, influencing the country's economy, borrowing, and interest rates.

a. Probability of default
b. Private money
c. Fractional-reserve banking
d. Reserve requirement

35. _____s are cash, evidence of an ownership interest in an entity or deliver, cash or another _____.

_____s can be categorized by form depending on whether they are cash instruments or derivative instruments:

- Cash instruments are _____s whose value is determined directly by markets. They can be divided into securities, which are readily transferable, and other cash instruments such as loans and deposits, where both borrower and lender have to agree on a transfer.
- Derivative instruments are _____s which derive their value from the value and characteristics of one or more underlying assets. They can be divided into exchange-traded derivatives and over-the-counter (OTC) derivatives.

Chapter 9. Global Money and Banking—Where Central Banks Fit into the World Economy

Alternatively, _____s can be categorized by 'asset class' depending on whether they are equity based (reflecting ownership of the issuing entity) or debt based (reflecting a loan the investor has made to the issuing entity.) If it is debt, it can be further categorised into short term (less than one year) or long term.

Foreign Exchange instruments and transactions are neither debt nor equity based and belong in their own category.

a. Municipal Bond Arbitrage
b. Financial instrument
c. Market liquidity
d. Fundamentally based indexes

36. _____s are financial contracts whose values are derived from the value of something else (known as the underlying.) The underlying value on which a _____ is based can be an asset (e.g., commodities, equities (stocks), residential mortgages, commercial real estate, loans, bonds), an index (e.g., interest rates, exchange rates, stock market indices, consumer price index (CPI) -- see inflation _____s), weather conditions bonds or other forms of credit.
    a. 100-year flood
    b. 130-30 fund
    c. Second derivative
    d. Derivative

37. The most common mechanism used to measure this increase in the money supply is typically called the _____. It calculates the maximum amount of money that an initial deposit can be expanded to with a given reserve ratio - such a factor is called a multiplier.

The _____, m, is the inverse of the reserve requirement, R:

$$m = \frac{1}{R}$$

This formula stems from the fact that the sum of the 'amount loaned out' column above can be expressed mathematically as a geometric series with a common ratio of 1 − R.

a. Fixed-income arbitrage
b. Kibbutz volunteers
c. Money multiplier
d. Flow to Equity-Approach

Chapter 9. Global Money and Banking—Where Central Banks Fit into the World Economy

38. In economics, _____ is the total amount of money available in an economy at a particular point in time. There are several ways to define 'money', but standard measures usually include currency in circulation and demand deposits.

_____ data are recorded and published, usually by the government or the central bank of the country.

a. Money supply
b. Veil of money
c. Neutrality of money
d. Velocity of money

39. Economics:

- _____, the desire to own something and the ability to pay for it
- _____ curve, a graphic representation of a _____ schedule
- _____ deposit, the money in checking accounts
- _____ pull theory, the theory that inflation occurs when _____ for goods and services exceeds existing supplies
- _____ schedule, a table that lists the quantity of a good a person will buy it each different price
- _____ side economics, the school of economics at believes government spending and tax cuts open economy by raising _____

a. McKesson ' Robbins scandal
b. Production
c. Variability
d. Demand

40. The _____ or gross domestic income (GDI), a basic measure of an economy's economic performance, is the market value of all final goods and services produced within the borders of a nation in a year. _____ can be defined in three ways, all of which are conceptually identical. First, it is equal to the total expenditures for all final goods and services produced within the country in a stipulated period of time (usually a 365-day year.)

a. Countercyclical
b. Gross domestic product
c. Market structure
d. Monopolistic competition

41. A variety of measures of _____ and output are used in economics to estimate total economic activity in a country or region, including gross domestic product (GDP), gross national product (GNP), and net _____

Chapter 9. Global Money and Banking—Where Central Banks Fit into the World Economy

There are three main ways of calculating these numbers; the output approach, the income approach and the expenditure approach. In theory, the three must yield the same, because total expenditures on goods and services must equal the total income paid to the producers (Gnational income), and that must also equal the total value of the output of goods and services (GNP.)

a. Gross world product
b. GNI per capita
c. National income
d. Volume index

42. In statistics, a _____ is a value that allows data to be measured over time in terms of some base period ussually through a price index in order to distinguish between changes in the money value of GNP which result from a change in prices and those which result from a change in physical output. It is the measure of the price level for some quantity. A _____ serves as a price index in which the effects of inflation are nulled.

a. Contingent employment
b. Deflator
c. Blanket order
d. Market microstructure

43. _____ in economics and business is the result of an exchange and from that trade we assign a numerical monetary value to a good, service or asset. If Alice trades Bob 4 apples for an orange, the _____ of an orange is 4 apples. Inversely, the _____ of an apple is 1/4 oranges.

a. Price
b. Price book
c. Premium pricing
d. Price war

44. _____ is a macroeconomic measure of the size of an economy adjusted for price changes and inflation. It measures in constant prices the output of final goods and services and incomes within an economy. The formula for its definition is [(Nominal GDP)/(GDP deflator)] x 100, however, it is not calculated in this way.

a. Bureau of Labor Statistics
b. Gross world product
c. Real gross domestic product
d. TED spread

45. An _____, in economics, is the amount by which the real Gross domestic product exceeds potential GDP. The real GDP is also known as GDP 'adjusted for inflation', 'constant prices' GDP or 'constant dollar' GDP, because it measures the aggregate output in a country's income accounts in a given year, expressed in base-year prices. On the other hand, the potential GDP is the quantity of real GDP when a country's economy is at full-employment.
   a. Inflationary gap
   b. ACEA agreement
   c. AD-IA Model
   d. ACCRA Cost of Living Index

46. The _____ is a treaty of the World Trade Organization (WTO) that entered into force in January 1995 as a result of the Uruguay Round negotiations. The treaty was created to extend the multilateral trading system to service sector, in the same way the General Agreement on Tariffs and Trade (GATT) provides such a system for merchandise trade.

All members of the WTO are signatories to the GATS.

   a. Dutch-Scandinavian Economic Pact
   b. General Agreement on Tariffs and Trade
   c. GATT
   d. General Agreement on Trade in Services

47. A _____ is a hypothetical measure of overall prices for some set of goods and services, in a given region during a given interval, normalized relative to some base set. Typically, a _____ is approximated with a price index.

The classical dichotomy is the assumption that there is a relatively clean distinction between overall increases or decreases in prices and underlying, e;reale; economic variables.

   a. Price level
   b. Price elasticity of supply
   c. Discretionary spending
   d. Discouraged worker

48. In economics, _____ is the total demand for final goods and services in the economy (Y) at a given time and price level. It is the amount of goods and services in the economy that will be purchased at all possible price levels. This is the demand for the gross domestic product of a country when inventory levels are static.
   a. Aggregate supply
   b. Aggregation problem
   c. Aggregate expenditure
   d. Aggregate demand

49. In economics, _____ is the total supply of goods and services produced by a national economy during a specific time period. It is the total amount of goods and services in the economy available at all possible price levels.
   a. Aggregation problem
   b. Aggregate Supply
   c. Aggregate demand
   d. Aggregate expenditure

50. In finance, the _____s between two currencies specifies how much one currency is worth in terms of the other. It is the value of a foreign natione;s currency in terms of the home natione;s currency. For example an _____ of 102 Japanese yen to the United States dollar means that JPY 102 is worth the same as USD 1.
   a. ACCRA Cost of Living Index
   b. ACEA agreement
   c. Interbank market
   d. Exchange rate

51. The _____ is where currency trading takes place. It is where banks and other official institutions facilitate the buying and selling of foreign currencies. FX transactions typically involve one party purchasing a quantity of one currency in exchange for paying a quantity of another.
   a. Covered interest arbitrage
   b. Currency swap
   c. Floating currency
   d. Foreign exchange market

Chapter 10. Can Globalization Lift All Boats?

1. Economics:

   - _____, the desire to own something and the ability to pay for it
   - _____ curve, a graphic representation of a _____ schedule
   - _____ deposit, the money in checking accounts
   - _____ pull theory, the theory that inflation occurs when _____ for goods and services exceeds existing supplies
   - _____ schedule, a table that lists the quantity of a good a person will buy it each different price
   - _____ side economics, the school of economics at believes government spending and tax cuts open economy by raising _____

   a. McKesson ' Robbins scandal
   b. Variability
   c. Production
   d. Demand

2. The _____, a unit of the United States Department of Labor, is the principal fact-finding agency for the U.S. government in the broad field of labor economics and statistics. The BLS is an independent national statistical agency that collects, processes, analyzes, and disseminates essential statistical data to the American public, the U.S. Congress, other Federal agencies, State and local governments, business, and labor representatives. The BLS also serves as a statistical resource to the Department of Labor.

   a. Gross world product
   b. Gross Regional Product
   c. Gross national product
   d. Bureau of Labor Statistics

3. In microeconomics, _____ is the extra revenue that an additional unit of product will bring. It is the additional income from selling one more unit of a good; sometimes equal to price. It can also be described as the change in total revenue/change in number of units sold.

   a. Reservation price
   b. Marginal revenue
   c. Long term
   d. Market demand schedule

4. The marginal revenue productivity theory of wages, also referred to as the _____ of labor, is the change in total revenue earned by a firm that results from employing one more unit of labor. It is a neoclassical model that determines, under some conditions, the optimal number of workers to employ at an exogenously determined market wage rate.

   The _____ of a worker is equal to the product of the marginal product of labor (MP) and the marginal revenue (MR), given by MR×MP = _____.

a. Marginal revenue productivity theory of wages
b. Coal depletion
c. Real prices and ideal prices
d. Marginal revenue product

5. This concept is also known as the law of diminishing marginal returns, the _____, or the law of increasing opportunity cost.

The concept of diminishing returns can be traced back to the concerns of early economists such as Johann Heinrich von Thünen, Turgot, Thomas Malthus and David Ricardo.

Suppose that one kilogram of seed applied to a plot of land of a fixed size produces one ton of crop.

a. Lang Law
b. Fair Labor Standards Act
c. Bennett Amendment
d. Law of increasing relative cost

6. In economics, the _____ or marginal physical product is the extra output produced by one more unit of an input (for instance, the difference in output when a firm's labour is increased from five to six units.) Assuming that no other inputs to production change, the _____ of a given input (X) can be expressed as:

_____ = $\Delta Y/\Delta X$ = (the change of Y)/(the change of X.)

-
  - o
    - Pending approval by Thomas Sowell***

In neoclassical economics, this is the mathematical derivative of the production function.... Note that the 'product' (Y) is typically defined ignoring external costs and benefits.

a. Labor problem
b. Productive capacity
c. Factor prices
d. Marginal product

7. In economics, the _____ also known as MPL or MPN is the change in output from hiring one additional unit of labor. It is the increase in output added by the last unit of labor. Assuming that no other inputs to production change, the marginal product of a given input (X) can be expressed as:

MP = ΔY/ΔX = (the change of Y)/(the change of X.)

a. Marginal product
b. Product Pipeline
c. Production function
d. Marginal product of labor

8. In economics, _____ refers to how the marginal contribution of a factor of production usually decreases as more of the factor is used. According to this relationship, in a production system with fixed and variable inputs, beyond some point, each additional unit of the variable input yields smaller and smaller increases in output. Conversely, producing one more unit of output costs more and more in variable inputs.

a. Diminishing returns
b. Derivatives law
c. Patent troll
d. Community property

9. _____ is a term in economics, where demand for one good or service occurs as a result of demand for another. This may occur as the former is a part of production of the second. For example, demand for coal leads to _____ for mining, as coal must be mined for coal to be consumed.

a. Leontief production function
b. Rate risk
c. Days Sales Outstanding
d. Derived demand

10. In economics, the _____ can be defined as the graph depicting the relationship between the price of a certain commodity, and the amount of it that consumers are willing and able to purchase at that given price. It is a graphic representation of a demand schedule. The _____ for all consumers together follows from the _____ of every individual consumer: the individual demands at each price are added together.

a. Cost curve
b. Wage curve
c. Kuznets curve
d. Demand curve

Chapter 10. Can Globalization Lift All Boats?

11. In economics, _____ refers to the ability of a party to produce a good or service using fewer real resources than another entity producing the same good or service..A party has an _____ when using the same input as another party, it can produce a greater output. Since _____ is determined by a simple comparison of labor productivities, it is possible for a a party to have no _____ in anything. It can be contrasted with the concept of comparative advantage which refers to the ability to produce a particular good at a lower opportunity cost.

   a. ACCRA Cost of Living Index
   b. Index number
   c. Absolute advantage
   d. International economics

12. _____ is a specific term used in companies' financial reporting from the company-whole point of view. Because that use excludes the effects of changing ownership interest, an economic measure of _____ is necessary for financial analysis from the shareholders' point of view

   _____ is defined by the Financial Accounting Standards Board, or FASB, as e;the change in equity [net assets] of a business enterprise during a period from transactions and other events and circumstances from nonowner sources. It includes all changes in equity during a period except those resulting from investments by owners and distributions to owners.e;

   _____ is the sum of net income and other items that must bypass the income statement because they have not been realized, including items like an unrealized holding gain or loss from available for sale securities and foreign currency translation gains or losses.

   a. Windfall gain
   b. Real income
   c. Net national income
   d. Comprehensive income

13. _____s are externalities of economic activity or processes upon those who are not directly involved in it. Odours from a rendering plant are negative _____s upon its neighbours; the beauty of a homeowner's flower garden is a positive _____ upon neighbours.

   In the same way, the economic benefits of increased trade are the _____s anticipated in the formation of multilateral alliances of many of the regional nation states: e.g. SARC (South Asian Regional Cooperation), ASpillover effectAN (Association of South East Asian Nations)

   In reference to psychology, the _____ is when other people's emotions affect the emotions of those around them.

a. Public good
b. Cobb-Douglas
c. Business sector
d. Spillover effect

14. The _____ is the market for securities, where companies and governments can raise longterm funds. It is a market in which money is lent for periods longer than a year. The _____ includes the stock market and the bond market.
a. Financial instrument
b. Performance attribution
c. Multi-family office
d. Capital market

15. _____ is the additional output resulting from the use of an additional unit of capital (ceteris paribus assuming all other factors are fixed.) It equals to 1 divided by the Incremental Capital-Output Ratio.
a. Buy-write
b. Loan officer
c. CAN SLIM
d. Marginal product of capital

16. _____ describes a deliberate attempt to interfere with the free and fair operation of the market and create artificial, false or misleading appearances with respect to the price of a security, commodity or currency. _____ is prohibited under Section 9(a)(2) of the Securities Exchange Act of 1934, and in Australia under Section s 1041A of the Corporations Act 2001. The Act defines _____ as transactions which create an artificial price or maintain an artificial price for a tradable security.
a. Legal monopoly
b. Managerial economics
c. Net domestic product
d. Market manipulation

17. _____ is the act of leaving one's native country or region to settle in another. It is the same as immigration but from the perspective of the country of origin. Human movement before the establishment of political boundaries or within one state, is termed migration.
a. ACCRA Cost of Living Index
b. AD-IA Model
c. ACEA agreement
d. Emigration

Chapter 10. Can Globalization Lift All Boats?   91

18. The _____ is an international organization that oversees the global financial system by following the macroeconomic policies of its member countries, in particular those with an impact on exchange rates and the balance of payments. It is an organization formed to stabilize international exchange rates and facilitate development. It also offers financial and technical assistance to its members, making it an international lender of last resort.

   a. ACCRA Cost of Living Index
   b. ACEA agreement
   c. Office of Thrift Supervision
   d. International Monetary Fund

19. A _____, reserve bank, or monetary authority is the entity responsible for the monetary policy of a country or of a group of member states. It is a bank that can lend money to other banks in times of need. Its primary responsibility is to maintain the stability of the national currency and money supply, but more active duties include controlling subsidized-loan interest rates, and acting as a lender of last resort to the banking sector during times of financial crisis (private banks often being integral to the national financial system.)

   a. 100-year flood
   b. Central bank
   c. 1921 recession
   d. 130-30 fund

20. _____ refers to the exchange of products belonging to the same industry. The term is usually applied to international trade, where the same kinds of goods and services are both imported and exported.

Examples of this kind of trade include automobiles, foodstuffs and beverages, computers and minerals.

   a. Incoterms
   b. Intrastat
   c. Import quota
   d. Intra-industry trade

21. The _____ is an important selective, mainly private, international organization designed by its founders to supervise and liberalize international trade. The organization officially commenced on 1 January 1995, under the Marrakesh Agreement, succeeding the 1947 General Agreement on Tariffs and Trade (GATT.)

The _____ deals with regulation of trade between participating countries; it provides a framework for negotiating and formalising trade agreements, and a dispute resolution process aimed at enforcing participants' adherence to _____ agreements which are signed by representatives of member governments and ratified by their parliaments.

Chapter 10. Can Globalization Lift All Boats?

a. Bio-energy village
b. Backus-Kehoe-Kydland consumption correlation puzzle
c. World Trade Organization
d. 2009 G-20 London summit protests

22. _____s is the social science that studies the production, distribution, and consumption of goods and services. The term _____s comes from the Ancient Greek οἰκονομία from οἶκος (oikos, 'house') + νόμος (nomos, 'custom' or 'law'), hence 'rules of the house(hold)'. Current _____ models developed out of the broader field of political economy in the late 19th century, owing to a desire to use an empirical approach more akin to the physical sciences.
   a. Economic
   b. Inflation
   c. Opportunity cost
   d. Energy economics

23. _____ is the development of economic wealth of countries or regions for the well-being of their inhabitants. It is the process by which a nation improves the economic, political, and social well being of its people. From a policy perspective, _____ can be defined as efforts that seek to improve the economic well-being and quality of life for a community by creating and/or retaining jobs and supporting or growing incomes and the tax base.
   a. Economic development
   b. Economic methodology
   c. Experimental economics
   d. Inflation

24. _____ is the economic policy of restraining trade between states, through methods such as tariffs on imported goods, restrictive quotas, and a variety of other restrictive government regulations designed to discourage imports, and prevent foreign take-over of local markets and companies. This policy is closely aligned with anti-globalization, and contrasts with free trade, where government barriers to trade are kept to a minimum. The term is mostly used in the context of economics, where _____ refers to policies or doctrines which 'protect' businesses and workers within a country by restricting or regulating trade with foreign nations.
   a. Protectionism
   b. Digital economy
   c. Knowledge economy
   d. Google economy

25. _____ is exchange of capital, goods, and services across international borders or territories. In most countries, it represents a significant share of gross domestic product (GDP.) While _____ has been present throughout much of history, its economic, social, and political importance has been on the rise in recent centuries.

a. Intra-industry trade
b. Incoterms
c. Import license
d. International trade

Chapter 11. Industrial Structure and Trade in the Global Economy Businesses without Borders

1. _____ is a field of economics that studies the strategic behavior of firms, the structure of markets and their interactions. The study of _____ adds to the perfectly competitive model real-world frictions such as limited information, transaction cost, cost of adjusting prices, government actions, and barriers to entry by new firms into a market. It then considers how firms are organized and how they compete.
    a. Industrial organization
    b. Economic ideology
    c. Inflation
    d. Economic

2. _____ are the forces that cause larger firms to produce goods and services at increased per-unit costs. They are less well known than what economists have long understood as 'economies of scale', the forces which enable larger firms to produce goods and services at reduced per-unit costs.

    Some of the forces which cause a diseconomy of scale are listed below:

    Ideally, all employees of a firm would have one-on-one communication with each other so they know exactly what the other workers are doing.

    a. Factors of production
    b. Marginal physical product
    c. Productive capacity
    d. Diseconomies of scale

3. _____, in microeconomics, are the cost advantages that a business obtains due to expansion. They are factors that cause a producere;s average cost per unit to fall as scale is increased. _____ is a long run concept and refers to reductions in unit cost as the size of a facility, or scale, increases.
    a. Economic production quantity
    b. Underinvestment employment relationship
    c. Economies of scale
    d. Isoquant

4. In economic models, the _____ time frame assumes no fixed factors of production. Firms can enter or leave the marketplace, and the cost (and availability) of land, labor, raw materials, and capital goods can be assumed to vary. In contrast, in the short-run time frame, certain factors are assumed to be fixed, because there is not sufficient time for them to change.
    a. Productivity world
    b. Price/performance ratio
    c. Diseconomies of scale
    d. Long-run

Chapter 11. Industrial Structure and Trade in the Global Economy Businesses without Borders

5. In economics, _____ refers to the ability of a party to produce a good or service using fewer real resources than another entity producing the same good or service..A party has an _____ when using the same input as another party, it can produce a greater output. Since _____ is determined by a simple comparison of labor productivities, it is possible for a a party to have no _____ in anything. It can be contrasted with the concept of comparative advantage which refers to the ability to produce a particular good at a lower opportunity cost.

   a. Absolute advantage
   b. Index number
   c. ACCRA Cost of Living Index
   d. International economics

6. In economics, _____ is equal to total cost divided by the number of goods produced (the output quantity, Q.) It is also equal to the sum of average variable costs (total variable costs divided by Q) plus average fixed costs (total fixed costs divided by Q.) _____s may be dependent on the time period considered (increasing production may be expensive or impossible in the short term, for example.)

   a. Average variable cost
   b. Average fixed cost
   c. Average cost
   d. Explicit cost

7. In economic theory, _____ is the competitive situation in any market where the conditions necessary for perfect competition are not satisfied. It is a market structure that does not meet the conditions of perfect competition.

Forms of _____ include:

- Monopoly, in which there is only one seller of a good.
- Oligopoly, in which there is a small number of sellers.
- Monopolistic competition, in which there are many sellers producing highly differentiated goods.
- Monopsony, in which there is only one buyer of a good.
- Oligopsony, in which there is a small number of buyers.

There may also be _____ in markets due to buyers or sellers lacking information about prices and the goods being traded.

There may also be _____ due to a time lag in a market.

   a. AD-IA Model
   b. ACCRA Cost of Living Index
   c. ACEA agreement
   d. Imperfect competition

Chapter 11. Industrial Structure and Trade in the Global Economy Businesses without Borders

8. In neoclassical economics and microeconomics, _____ describes the perfect being a market in which there are many small firms, all producing homogeneous goods. In the short term, such markets are productively inefficient as output will not occur where mc is equal to ac, but allocatively efficient, as output under _____ will always occur where mc is equal to mr, and therefore where mc equals ar. However, in the long term, such markets are both allocatively and productively efficient.

   a. Co-operative economics
   b. General equilibrium
   c. Perfect competition
   d. Law of supply

9. A _____, reserve bank, or monetary authority is the entity responsible for the monetary policy of a country or of a group of member states. It is a bank that can lend money to other banks in times of need. Its primary responsibility is to maintain the stability of the national currency and money supply, but more active duties include controlling subsidized-loan interest rates, and acting as a lender of last resort to the banking sector during times of financial crisis (private banks often being integral to the national financial system.)

   a. 100-year flood
   b. 130-30 fund
   c. 1921 recession
   d. Central bank

10. _____ refers to the exchange of products belonging to the same industry. The term is usually applied to international trade, where the same kinds of goods and services are both imported and exported.

    Examples of this kind of trade include automobiles, foodstuffs and beverages, computers and minerals.

    a. Incoterms
    b. Intra-industry trade
    c. Intrastat
    d. Import quota

11. _____ is a common market structure where many competing producers sell products that are differentiated from one another (ie. the products are substitutes, but are not exactly alike.) Many markets are monopolistically competitive, common examples include the markets for restaurants, cereal, clothing, shoes and service industries in large cities.

    a. Monopolistic competition
    b. Perfect competition
    c. Financial crisis
    d. Mathematical economics

Chapter 11. Industrial Structure and Trade in the Global Economy Businesses without Borders

12. _____s is the social science that studies the production, distribution, and consumption of goods and services. The term _____s comes from the Ancient Greek οἰκονομία from οἶκος (oikos, 'house') + νόμος (nomos, 'custom' or 'law'), hence 'rules of the house(hold)'. Current _____ models developed out of the broader field of political economy in the late 19th century, owing to a desire to use an empirical approach more akin to the physical sciences.
    a. Inflation
    b. Energy economics
    c. Opportunity cost
    d. Economic

13. In economics, _____ is the difference between a company's total revenue and its opportunity costs. It is the increase in wealth that an investor has from making an investment, taking into consideration all costs associated with that investment including the opportunity cost of capital.

    Profit is the factor income of the entrepreneur.

    a. Accounting profit
    b. Economic profit
    c. Operating profit
    d. ACCRA Cost of Living Index

14. In economics and finance, _____ is the change in total cost that arises when the quantity produced changes by one unit. It is the cost of producing one more unit of a good. Mathematically, the _____ function is expressed as the first derivative of the total cost (TC) function with respect to quantity (Q.)
    a. Variable cost
    b. Quality costs
    c. Khozraschyot
    d. Marginal cost

15. In microeconomics, _____ is the extra revenue that an additional unit of product will bring. It is the additional income from selling one more unit of a good; sometimes equal to price. It can also be described as the change in total revenue/change in number of units sold.
    a. Market demand schedule
    b. Reservation price
    c. Long term
    d. Marginal revenue

Chapter 11. Industrial Structure and Trade in the Global Economy Businesses without Borders

16. In economics, the concept of the _____ refers to the decision-making time frame of a firm in which at least one factor of production is fixed. Costs which are fixed in the _____ have no impact on a firms decisions. For example a firm can raise output by increasing the amount of labour through overtime.

   a. Short-run
   b. Product Pipeline
   c. Hicks-neutral technical change
   d. Productivity model

17. _____ in its classic form is defined as a company from one country making a physical investment into building a factory in another country. It is the establishment of an enterprise by a foreigner. Its definition can be extended to include investments made to acquire lasting interest in enterprises operating outside of the economy of the investor.

   a. Non-governmental organization
   b. Financial Stability Forum
   c. Foreign direct investment
   d. Federal Deposit Insurance Corporation

18. In economics and especially in the theory of competition, _____ are obstacles in the path of a firm that make it difficult to enter a given market.

   _____ are the source of a firm's pricing power - the ability of a firm to raise prices without losing all its customers.

   The term refers to hindrances that an individual may face while trying to gain entrance into a profession or trade.

   a. Limit price
   b. Social dumping
   c. Group boycott
   d. Barriers to entry

19. _____ in its literal sense is the process of transformation of local or regional phenomena into global ones. It can be described as a process by which the people of the world are unified into a single society and function together.

   This process is a combination of economic, technological, sociocultural and political forces.

   a. Globally Integrated Enterprise
   b. Global Cosmopolitanism
   c. Helsinki Process on Globalisation and Democracy
   d. Globalization

Chapter 11. Industrial Structure and Trade in the Global Economy Businesses without Borders

20. The _____ is a trilateral trade bloc in North America created by the governments of the United States, Canada, and Mexico. The agreement creating the trade bloc came into force on January 1, 1994. It superseded the Canada-United States Free Trade Agreement between the U.S. and Canada.
    a. Demand-side technologies
    b. Federal Reserve Bank Notes
    c. Case-Shiller Home Price Indices
    d. North American Free Trade Agreement

21. In microeconomics, _____ is quite simply the conversion of inputs into outputs. It is an economic process that uses resources to create a good or service that is suitable for exchange. This can include manufacturing, storing, shipping, and packaging.
    a. MET
    b. Production
    c. Solved
    d. Red Guards

22. _____ is the advantage gained by the initial occupant of a market segment. This advantage may stem from the fact that the first entrant can gain control of resources that followers may not be able to match. Sometimes the first mover is not able to capitalise on its advantage, leaving the opportunity for another firm to gain second-mover advantage.
    a. First-mover advantage
    b. Business engineering
    c. Cross-docking
    d. Continuous Improvement Process

23. In economics, a _____ exists when a specific individual or enterprise has sufficient control over a particular product or service to determine significantly the terms on which other individuals shall have access to it. Monopolies are thus characterized by a lack of economic competition for the good or service that they provide and a lack of viable substitute goods. The verb 'monopolize' refers to the process by which a firm gains persistently greater market share than what is expected under perfect competition.
    a. 130-30 fund
    b. 100-year flood
    c. 1921 recession
    d. Monopoly

24. An _____ is a market form in which a market or industry is dominated by a small number of sellers (oligopolists.) Because there are few participants in this type of market, each oligopolist is aware of the actions of the others. The decisions of one firm influence, and are influenced by, the decisions of other firms.

Chapter 11. Industrial Structure and Trade in the Global Economy Businesses without Borders

a. Oligopoly
b. ACEA agreement
c. Oligopsony
d. ACCRA Cost of Living Index

25. The phrase _____ refers to the aspect of corporate strategy, corporate finance and management dealing with the buying, selling and combining of different companies that can aid, finance, or help a growing company in a given industry grow rapidly without having to create another business entity.

An acquisition, also known as a takeover or a buyout, is the buying of one company (the 'target') by another. An acquisition may be friendly or hostile.

a. Peace dividend
b. Political economy
c. Productive and unproductive labour
d. Mergers and acquisitions

26. The phrase _____ and acquisitions refers to the aspect of corporate strategy, corporate finance and management dealing with the buying, selling and combining of different companies that can aid, finance, or help a growing company in a given industry grow rapidly without having to create another business entity.

An acquisition, also known as a takeover or a buyout, is the buying of one company (the 'target') by another. An acquisition may be friendly or hostile.

a. Political economy
b. Peace dividend
c. Differential accumulation
d. Mergers

27. In economics, the _____ of an industry is used as an indicator of the relative size of firms in relation to the industry as a whole. It is calculated as the sum of the percent market share of the top n industries. This may also assist in determining the market structure of the industry.

a. Monopolization
b. Pacman conjecture
c. Quasi-rent
d. Concentration ratio

Chapter 11. Industrial Structure and Trade in the Global Economy Businesses without Borders

28. In economics, _____ is a function of the number of firms and their respective shares of the total production (alternatively, total capacity or total reserves) in a market. Alternative terms are Industry concentration and Seller concentration.

_____ is related to the concept of industrial concentration, which concerns the distribution of production within an industry, as opposed to a market.

a. Decartelization
b. Monopolization
c. Quasi-rent
d. Market concentration

29. A _____ is an expression that compares quantities relative to each other. The most common examples involve two quantities, but any number of quantities can be compared. _____s are represented mathematically by separating each quantity with a colon, for example the _____ 2:3, which is read as the _____ 'two to three'.

a. 100-year flood
b. 130-30 fund
c. Y-intercept
d. Ratio

30. In competition law the _____ defines the market in which one or more goods compete. Therefore, the _____ defines whether two or more products can be considered substitute goods and whether they constitute a particular and separate market for competition analysis.

The _____ combines the product market and the geographic market, defined as follows:

1. A relevant product market comprises all those products and/or services which are regarded as interchangeable or substitutable by the consumer by reason of the products' characteristics, their prices and their intended use;
2. A relevant geographic market comprises the area in which the firms concerned are involved in the supply of products or services and in which the conditions of competition are sufficiently homogeneous.

The notion of _____ is used in order to identify the products and undertakings which are directly competing in a business. Therefore, the _____ is the market where the competition takes place.

a. Community property
b. Greenfield agreement
c. Relevant market
d. Competition law

Chapter 11. Industrial Structure and Trade in the Global Economy Businesses without Borders

31. Competition law, known in the United States as _____ law, has three main elements:

- prohibiting agreements or practices that restrict free trading and competition between business entities. This includes in particular the repression of cartels.
- banning abusive behaviour by a firm dominating a market, or anti-competitive practices that tend to lead to such a dominant position. Practices controlled in this way may include predatory pricing, tying, price gouging, refusal to deal, and many others.
- supervising the mergers and acquisitions of large corporations, including some joint ventures. Transactions that are considered to threaten the competitive process can be prohibited altogether, or approved subject to 'remedies' such as an obligation to divest part of the merged business or to offer licences or access to facilities to enable other businesses to continue competing.

The substance and practice of competition law varies from jurisdiction to jurisdiction. Protecting the interests of consumers (consumer welfare) and ensuring that entrepreneurs have an opportunity to compete in the market economy are often treated as important objectives. Competition law is closely connected with law on deregulation of access to markets, state aids and subsidies, the privatisation of state owned assets and the establishment of independent sector regulators. In recent decades, competition law has been viewed as a way to provide better public services.

a. United Kingdom competition law
b. Anti-Inflation Act
c. Antitrust
d. Intellectual property law

32. _____, known in the United States as antitrust law, has three main elements:

- prohibiting agreements or practices that restrict free trading and competition between business entities. This includes in particular the repression of cartels.
- banning abusive behaviour by a firm dominating a market, or anti-competitive practices that tend to lead to such a dominant position. Practices controlled in this way may include predatory pricing, tying, price gouging, refusal to deal, and many others.
- supervising the mergers and acquisitions of large corporations, including some joint ventures. Transactions that are considered to threaten the competitive process can be prohibited altogether, or approved subject to 'remedies' such as an obligation to divest part of the merged business or to offer licences or access to facilities to enable other businesses to continue competing.

The substance and practice of _____ varies from jurisdiction to jurisdiction. Protecting the interests of consumers (consumer welfare) and ensuring that entrepreneurs have an opportunity to compete in the market economy are often treated as important objectives. _____ is closely connected with law on deregulation of access to markets, state aids and subsidies, the privatisation of state owned assets and the establishment of independent sector regulators. In recent decades, _____ has been viewed as a way to provide better public services.

Chapter 11. Industrial Structure and Trade in the Global Economy Businesses without Borders

a. Hostile work environment
b. Due diligence
c. Competition law
d. Fee simple

33. _____ in economics and business is the result of an exchange and from that trade we assign a numerical monetary value to a good, service or asset. If Alice trades Bob 4 apples for an orange, the _____ of an orange is 4 apples. Inversely, the _____ of an apple is 1/4 oranges.
    a. Price war
    b. Price book
    c. Premium pricing
    d. Price

34. _____ exists when sales of identical goods or services are transacted at different prices from the same provider. In a theoretical market with perfect information, no transaction costs or prohibition on secondary exchange (or re-selling) to prevent arbitrage, _____ can only be a feature of monopoly and oligopoly markets, where market power can be exercised. Otherwise, the moment the seller tries to sell the same good at different prices, the buyer at the lower price can arbitrage by selling to the consumer buying at the higher price but with a tiny discount.
    a. Loss leader
    b. Transfer pricing
    c. Price discrimination
    d. Lerner Index

35. _____ is the practice of selling a product or service at a very low price, intending to drive competitors out of the market, or create barriers to entry for potential new competitors. If competitors or potential competitors cannot sustain equal or lower prices without losing money, they go out of business or choose not to enter the business. The predatory merchant then has fewer competitors or is even a de facto monopoly, and can then raise prices above what the market would otherwise bear.
    a. Third line forcing
    b. Group boycott
    c. Restraint of trade
    d. Predatory pricing

36. _____ is one of the four Ps of the marketing mix. The other three aspects are product, promotion, and place. It is also a key variable in microeconomic price allocation theory.

a. Point of total assumption
b. Guaranteed Maximum Price
c. Premium pricing
d. Pricing

Chapter 12. The Public Sector in the Global Economy

1. _____ is a broad label that refers to any individuals or households that use goods and services generated within the economy. The concept of a _____ is used in different contexts, so that the usage and significance of the term may vary.

Typically when business people and economists talk of _____s they are talking about person as _____, an aggregated commodity item with little individuality other than that expressed in the buy/not-buy decision.

a. 100-year flood
b. 130-30 fund
c. 1921 recession
d. Consumer

2. _____ laws are designed to ensure fair competition and the free flow of truthful information in the marketplace. The laws are designed to prevent businesses that engage in fraud or specified unfair practices from gaining an advantage over competitors and may provide additional protection for the weak and unable to take care of themselves. _____ laws are a form of government regulation which protects the interests of consumers.

a. History of minimum wage
b. Dow Jones Industrial Average
c. Global warming
d. Consumer protection

3. _____, anti-selection insurance, statistics, and risk management. It refers to a market process in which 'bad' results occur when buyers and sellers have asymmetric information (i.e. access to different information): the 'bad' products or customers are more likely to be selected. A bank that sets one price for all its checking account customers runs the risk of being adversely selected against by its low-balance, high-activity (and hence least profitable) customers.

a. ACCRA Cost of Living Index
b. AD-IA Model
c. ACEA agreement
d. Adverse selection

4. _____ is the prospect that a party insulated from risk may behave differently from the way it would behave if it were fully exposed to the risk. In insurance, _____ that occurs without conscious or malicious action is called morale hazard.

_____ is related to information asymmetry, a situation in which one party in a transaction has more information than another.

Chapter 12. The Public Sector in the Global Economy

   a. 100-year flood
   b. Moral hazard
   c. 1921 recession
   d. 130-30 fund

5. The _____ is an economic and political union of 27 member states, located primarily in Europe. It was established by the Treaty of Maastricht on 1 November 1993, upon the foundations of the pre-existing European Economic Community. With a population of almost 500 million, the _____ generates an estimated 30% share (US$18.4 trillion in 2008) of the nominal gross world product.
   a. European Court of Justice
   b. ACCRA Cost of Living Index
   c. ACEA agreement
   d. European Union

6. _____ is the economic policy of restraining trade between states, through methods such as tariffs on imported goods, restrictive quotas, and a variety of other restrictive government regulations designed to discourage imports, and prevent foreign take-over of local markets and companies. This policy is closely aligned with anti-globalization, and contrasts with free trade, where government barriers to trade are kept to a minimum. The term is mostly used in the context of economics, where _____ refers to policies or doctrines which 'protect' businesses and workers within a country by restricting or regulating trade with foreign nations.
   a. Google economy
   b. Digital economy
   c. Knowledge economy
   d. Protectionism

7. In economics, an _____ is any good (e.g. a commodity) or service brought into one country from another country in a legitimate fashion, typically for use in trade. It is a good that is brought in from another country for sale. _____ goods or services are provided to domestic consumers by foreign producers. An _____ in the receiving country is an export to the sending country.
   a. Import
   b. Import quota
   c. Incoterms
   d. Economic integration

8. _____ are legal property rights over creations of the mind, both artistic and commercial, and the corresponding fields of law. Under _____ law, owners are granted certain exclusive rights to a variety of intangible assets, such as musical, literary, and artistic works; ideas, discoveries and inventions; and words, phrases, symbols, and designs. Common types of _____ include copyrights, trademarks, patents, industrial design rights and trade secrets.

a. Intellectual property
b. Expedited Funds Availability Act
c. Independent contractor
d. Ease of Doing Business Index

9. A _____ is a set of exclusive rights granted by a state to an inventor or his assignee for a limited period of time in exchange for a disclosure of an invention.

The procedure for granting _____s, the requirements placed on the _____ee and the extent of the exclusive rights vary widely between countries according to national laws and international agreements. Typically, however, a _____ application must include one or more claims defining the invention which must be new, inventive, and useful or industrially applicable.

a. Bank regulation
b. Long service leave
c. Bona fide occupational qualification
d. Patent

10. A _____ is the exclusive authority to determine how a resource is used, whether that resource is owned by government or by individuals. All economic goods have a _____s attribute. This attribute has three broad components

1. The right to use the good
2. The right to earn income from the good
3. The right to transfer the good to others

The concept of _____s as used by economists and legal scholars are related but distinct. The distinction is largely seen in the economists' focus on the ability of an individual or collective to control the use of the good.

a. High-reeve
b. Post-sale restraint
c. Holder in due course
d. Property right

108   Chapter 12. The Public Sector in the Global Economy

11. A _____ is:

- Rewrite _____, in generative grammar and computer science
- Standardization, a formal and widely-accepted statement, fact, definition, or qualification
- Operation, a determinate _____ for performing a mathematical operation and obtaining a certain result (Mathematics, Logic)
    - Unary operation
    - Binary operation
- _____ of inference, a function from sets of formulae to formulae (Mathematics, Logic)
- _____ of thumb, principle with broad application that is not intended to be strictly accurate or reliable for every situation. Also often simply referred to as a _____
- Moral, an atomic element of a moral code for guiding choices in human behavior
- Heuristic, a quantized '_____' which shows a tendency or probability for successful function
- A regulation, as in sports
- A Production _____, as in computer science
- Procedural law, a _____ set governing the application of laws to cases
    - A law, which may informally be called a '_____'
    - A court ruling, a decision by a court
- In the U.S. Government, a regulation mandated by Congress, but written or expanded upon by the Executive Branch.
- Norm (sociology), an informal but widely accepted _____, concept, truth, definition, or qualification (social norms, legal norms, coding norms)
- Norm (philosophy), a kind of sentence or a reason to act, feel or believe
- 'Rulership' is the concept of governance by a government:
    - Military _____, governance by a military body
    - Monastic _____, a collection of precepts that guides the life of monks or nuns in a religious order where the superior holds the place of Christ
- Slide _____

- '_____,' a song by Ayumi Hamasaki
- '_____,' a song by rapper Nas
- '_____s,' an album by the band The Whitest Boy Alive
- _____s: Pyaar Ka Superhit Formula, a 2003 Bollywood film
- ruler, an instrument for measuring lengths
- _____, a component of an astrolabe, circumferator or similar instrument
- The _____s, a bestselling self-help book
- _____ Project (Run Up-to-date Linux Everywhere), a project that aims to use up-to-date Linux software on old PCs
- _____ engine, a software system that helps managing business _____s
- Ja _____, a hip hop artist
    - R.U.L.E., a 2005 greatest hits album by rapper Ja _____
- '_____s,' a KMFDM song

Chapter 12. The Public Sector in the Global Economy

a. Technocracy
b. Demand
c. Procter ' Gamble
d. Rule

12. In economics, a _____ exists when the production or use of goods and services by the market is not efficient. That is, there exists another outcome where all involved can be made better off. _____s can be viewed as scenarios where individuals' pursuit of pure self-interest leads to results that are not efficient - that can be improved upon from the societal point-of-view.
   a. Fixed exchange rate
   b. Financial economics
   c. Market failure
   d. General equilibrium

13. In economics, a _____ is a good that is non-rivaled and non-excludable. This means, respectively, that consumption of the good by one individual does not reduce availability of the good for consumption by others; and that no one can be effectively excluded from using the good. In the real world, there may be no such thing as an absolutely non-rivaled and non-excludable good; but economists think that some goods approximate the concept closely enough for the analysis to be economically useful.
   a. Happiness economics
   b. Neoclassical synthesis
   c. Public good
   d. Demand-pull theory

14. A _____ is an object whose consumption increases the utility of the consumer, for which the quantity demanded exceeds the quantity supplied at zero price. _____s are usually modeled as having diminishing marginal utility. The first individual purchase has high utility; the second has less.
   a. Merit good
   b. Composite good
   c. Pie method
   d. Good

15. The _____ is an important selective, mainly private, international organization designed by its founders to supervise and liberalize international trade. The organization officially commenced on 1 January 1995, under the Marrakesh Agreement, succeeding the 1947 General Agreement on Tariffs and Trade (GATT.)

The _____ deals with regulation of trade between participating countries; it provides a framework for negotiating and formalising trade agreements, and a dispute resolution process aimed at enforcing participants' adherence to _____ agreements which are signed by representatives of member governments and ratified by their parliaments.

   a. Backus-Kehoe-Kydland consumption correlation puzzle
   b. Bio-energy village
   c. 2009 G-20 London summit protests
   d. World Trade Organization

16.   A _____ is a good that has the three following properties :

- It is non-rivalrous. Consumption of this good by anyone does not reduce the quantity available to other agents.
- It is non-excludable. It is impossible to prevent anyone from consuming that good.
- It is available worldwide.

This concept is an extension of Samuelson's notion of public goods to the economics of globalisation.

The theoretical concept of public goods does not distinguish with regard to the geographical region in which a good may be produced or consumed. However some theorists (such as Inge Kaul) use the term _____ to mean a public good which is non-rival and non-excludable throughout the whole world, as opposed to a public good which exists in just one national area. Knowledge is a canonical example of a _____.[Joseph E. Stiglitz, Knowledge as a _____ in _____ s, ISBN 978-0-19-513052-2</ref>.]

   a. Black-Litterman model
   b. Community indifference curve
   c. Monopoly price
   d. Global public good

17.   The concept of a _____ introduced in economics introduced by Richard Musgrave (1957, 1959) is a commodity which is judged that an individual or society should have on the basis of some concept of need, rather than ability and willingness to pay. The term is, perhaps, less often used today than it was in the 1960s to 1980s but the concept still lies behind many economic actions by governments which are not performed specifically for financial reasons or by supporting incomes (eg via tax rebates.) Examples include the provision of food stamps to support nutrition, the delivery of health services to improve quality of life and reduce morbidity, subsidized housing and arguably education.

Chapter 12. The Public Sector in the Global Economy

a. Private good
b. Final good
c. Positional goods
d. Merit good

18. In economics, a common-pool resource, alternatively termed a _____ resource, is a particular type of good consisting of a natural or human-made resource system, the size or characteristics of which makes it costly, but not impossible, to exclude potential beneficiaries from obtaining benefits from its use. Unlike pure public goods, common pool resources face problems of congestion or overuse, because they are subtractable. A common-pool resource typically consists of a core resource, which defines the stock variable, while providing a limited quantity of extractable fringe units, which defines the flow variable.

a. Price-cap regulation
b. Common-pool resource
c. Government monopoly
d. Common property

19. Economics:

- _____ ,the desire to own something and the ability to pay for it
- _____ curve,a graphic representation of a _____ schedule
- _____ deposit, the money in checking accounts
- _____ pull theory,the theory that inflation occurs when _____ for goods and services exceeds existing supplies
- _____ schedule,a table that lists the quantity of a good a person will buy it each different price
- _____ side economics,the school of economics at believes government spending and tax cuts open economy by raising _____

a. Demand
b. Production
c. McKesson ' Robbins scandal
d. Variability

20. _____s is the social science that studies the production, distribution, and consumption of goods and services. The term _____s comes from the Ancient Greek oá¼°κονομῑα from oá¼¶κος (oikos, 'house') + vÏŒμος (nomos, 'custom' or 'law'), hence 'rules of the house(hold)'. Current _____ models developed out of the broader field of political economy in the late 19th century, owing to a desire to use an empirical approach more akin to the physical sciences.

a. Economic
b. Energy economics
c. Inflation
d. Opportunity cost

21. _____ is exchange of capital, goods, and services across international borders or territories. In most countries, it represents a significant share of gross domestic product (GDP.) While _____ has been present throughout much of history , its economic, social, and political importance has been on the rise in recent centuries.

a. Incoterms
b. Intra-industry trade
c. Import license
d. International trade

22. To _____ is to impose a financial charge or other levy upon a taxpayer by a state or the functional equivalent of a state.

_____es are also imposed by many subnational entities. _____es consist of direct _____ or indirect _____, and may be paid in money or as its labour equivalent (often but not always unpaid.)

a. 1921 recession
b. 100-year flood
c. 130-30 fund
d. Tax

23. _____ are the income that is gained by governments because of taxation of the people.

Just as there are different types of tax, the form in which _____ is collected also differs; furthermore, the agency that collects the tax may not be part of central government, but may be an alternative third-party licenced to collect tax which they themselves will use. For example:

- In the UK, the DVLA collects road tax, which is then passed on the treasury.

_____s on purchases can come from two forms: 'tax' itself is a percentage of the price added to the purchase (such as sales tax in US states, or VAT in the UK), while 'duty' is a fixed amount added to the purchase price (such as is commonly found on cigarettes.) In order to calculate the total tax raised from these sales, we must work out the effective tax rate multiplied by the quantity supplied.

Chapter 12. The Public Sector in the Global Economy

a. Taxable wage
b. Tax and spend
c. Taxation as slavery
d. Tax revenue

24. To tax is to impose a financial charge or other levy upon a taxpayer by a state or the functional equivalent of a state. _____ are also imposed by many subnational entities. _____ consist of direct tax or indirect tax, and may be paid in money or as its labour equivalent (often but not always unpaid.)

a. Taxes
b. 100-year flood
c. 1921 recession
d. 130-30 fund

25. A _____ is a general term that describes any government policy or regulation that restricts international trade. The barriers can take many forms, including the following terms that include many restrictions in international trade within multiple countries that import and export any items of trade.

- Import duty
- Import licenses
- Export licenses
- Import quotas
- Tariffs
- Subsidies
- Non-tariff barriers to trade
- Voluntary Export Restraints
- Local Content Requirements
- Embargo

Most _____s work on the same principle: the imposition of some sort of cost on trade that raises the price of the traded products. If two or more nations repeatedly use _____s against each other, then a trade war results.

a. Certificate of origin
b. National Foreign Trade Council
c. Global financial system
d. Trade barrier

26. _____ exists when governments are encouraged to lower fiscal burdens to either encourage the inflow of productive resources or discourage the exodus of those resources. Often, this means a governmental strategy of attracting foreign direct investment, foreign indirect investment (financial investment), and high value human resources by minimizing the overall taxation level and/or special tax preferences, creating a comparative advantage.

Although often presented as a benefit for capital, _____ is generally a central part of a government policy for improving the lot of labour by creating well-paid jobs (often in countries or regions with very limited job prospects.)

   a. Taxable wage
   b. Tax competition
   c. Tax brackets
   d. Privatized tax collection

Chapter 13. Rules versus Discretion—Can Policymakers Stick to Their Promises?   115

1. In economics, _____ is a rise in the general level of prices of goods and services in an economy over a period of time. When the general price level rises, each unit of currency buys fewer goods and services; consequently, _____ is also a decline in the real value of money--a loss of purchasing power in the medium of exchange which is also the monetary unit of account in the economy. A chief measure of general price-level _____ is the general _____ rate, which is the percentage change in a general price index (normally the Consumer Price Index) over time.
   a. Opportunity cost
   b. Inflation
   c. Economic
   d. Energy economics

2. A _____, reserve bank, or monetary authority is the entity responsible for the monetary policy of a country or of a group of member states. It is a bank that can lend money to other banks in times of need. Its primary responsibility is to maintain the stability of the national currency and money supply, but more active duties include controlling subsidized-loan interest rates, and acting as a lender of last resort to the banking sector during times of financial crisis (private banks often being integral to the national financial system.)
   a. 130-30 fund
   b. 100-year flood
   c. 1921 recession
   d. Central bank

3. _____ is an economic theory that holds that the prosperity of a nation is dependent upon its supply of capital, and that the global volume of international trade is 'unchangeable.' Economic assets or capital, are represented by bullion (gold, silver, and trade value) held by the state, which is best increased through a positive balance of trade with other nations (exports minus imports.) _____ suggests that the ruling government should advance these goals by playing a protectionist role in the economy; by encouraging exports and discouraging imports, notably through the use of tariffs and subsidies.

   _____ was the dominant school of thought throughout the early modern period (from the 16th to the 18th century.)

   a. Mercantilism
   b. Consumer theory
   c. Nominal value
   d. General equilibrium theory

4. _____ is the process by which the government, central bank (ii) availability of money, and (iii) cost of money or rate of interest, in order to attain a set of objectives oriented towards the growth and stability of the economy. Monetary theory provides insight into how to craft optimal _____.

   _____ is referred to as either being an expansionary policy where an expansionary policy increases the total supply of money in the economy, and a contractionary policy decreases the total money supply.

a. 1921 recession
b. 130-30 fund
c. 100-year flood
d. Monetary policy

Chapter 13. Rules versus Discretion—Can Policymakers Stick to Their Promises? 117

5. A _____ is:

- Rewrite _____, in generative grammar and computer science
- Standardization, a formal and widely-accepted statement, fact, definition, or qualification
- Operation, a determinate _____ for performing a mathematical operation and obtaining a certain result (Mathematics, Logic)
    - Unary operation
    - Binary operation
- _____ of inference, a function from sets of formulae to formulae (Mathematics, Logic)
- _____ of thumb, principle with broad application that is not intended to be strictly accurate or reliable for every situation. Also often simply referred to as a _____
- Moral, an atomic element of a moral code for guiding choices in human behavior
- Heuristic, a quantized '_____' which shows a tendency or probability for successful function
- A regulation, as in sports
- A Production _____, as in computer science
- Procedural law, a _____ set governing the application of laws to cases
    - A law, which may informally be called a '_____'
    - A court ruling, a decision by a court
- In the U.S. Government, a regulation mandated by Congress, but written or expanded upon by the Executive Branch.
- Norm (sociology), an informal but widely accepted _____, concept, truth, definition, or qualification (social norms, legal norms, coding norms)
- Norm (philosophy), a kind of sentence or a reason to act, feel or believe
- 'Rulership' is the concept of governance by a government:
    - Military _____, governance by a military body
    - Monastic _____, a collection of precepts that guides the life of monks or nuns in a religious order where the superior holds the place of Christ
- Slide _____

- '_____,' a song by Ayumi Hamasaki
- '_____,' a song by rapper Nas
- '_____s,' an album by the band The Whitest Boy Alive
- _____s: Pyaar Ka Superhit Formula, a 2003 Bollywood film
- ruler, an instrument for measuring lengths
- _____, a component of an astrolabe, circumferator or similar instrument
- The _____s, a bestselling self-help book
- _____ Project (Run Up-to-date Linux Everywhere), a project that aims to use up-to-date Linux software on old PCs
- _____ engine, a software system that helps managing business _____s
- Ja _____, a hip hop artist
    - R.U.L.E., a 2005 greatest hits album by rapper Ja _____
- '_____s,' a KMFDM song

Chapter 13. Rules versus Discretion—Can Policymakers Stick to Their Promises?

   a. Technocracy
   b. Demand
   c. Procter ' Gamble
   d. Rule

6. A _____ is a situation that involves losing one quality or aspect of something in return for gaining another quality or aspect. It implies a decision to be made with full comprehension of both the upside and downside of a particular choice.

In economics the term is expressed as opportunity cost, referring the most preferred alternative given up.

   a. Whitemail
   b. Nonmarket
   c. Friedman-Savage utility function
   d. Trade-off

7. _____ is a term used to described a tendency or preference towards a particular perspective, ideology or result, especially when the tendency interferes with the ability to be impartial, unprejudiced, or objective. The term _____ed is used to describe an action, judgment, or other outcome influenced by a prejudged perspective. It is also used to refer to a person or body of people whose actions or judgments exhibit _____.

   a. 130-30 fund
   b. 100-year flood
   c. 1921 recession
   d. Bias

8. _____ refers to the objective and subjective components of the believability of a source or message.

Traditionally, _____ has two key components: trustworthiness and expertise, which both have objective and subjective components. Trustworthiness is a based more on subjective factors, but can include objective measurements such as established reliability.

   a. 1921 recession
   b. 130-30 fund
   c. Credibility
   d. 100-year flood

Chapter 13. Rules versus Discretion—Can Policymakers Stick to Their Promises? 119

9. In economics, _____ describes a situation where a decision-maker's preferences change over time, such that what is preferred at one point in time is inconsistent with what is preferred at another point in time. It is often easiest to think about preferences over time in this context by thinking of decision-makers as being made up of many different 'selves', with each self representing the decision-maker at a different point in time. So, for example, there is my today self, my tomorrow self, my next Tuesday self, my year from now self, etc.
   a. Cheap talk
   b. Bondareva-Shapley theorem
   c. Graph continuous
   d. Dynamic inconsistency

10. In economics, the _____ is a measure of inflation, the rate of increase of a price index (for example, a consumer price index.)It is the percentage rate of change in price level over time. The rate of decrease in the purchasing power of money is approximately equal.

    It's used to calculate the real interest rate, as well as real increases in wages, and official measurements of this rate act as input variables to COLA adjustments and Inflation derivatives prices.

    a. Interest rate option
    b. Inflation rate
    c. Equity value
    d. Edgeworth paradox

11. Wisconsin originated the idea of _____ in the U.S. in 1932. In the United States, there are 50 state _____ programs plus one each in the District of Columbia and Puerto Rico. Through the Social Security Act of 1935, the Federal Government of the United States effectively coerced the individual states into adopting _____ plans.
    a. ACEA agreement
    b. ACCRA Cost of Living Index
    c. AD-IA Model
    d. Unemployment insurance

12. _____, in law and economics, is a form of risk management primarily used to hedge against the risk of a contingent loss. _____ is defined as the equitable transfer of the risk of a loss, from one entity to another, in exchange for a premium, and can be thought of as a guaranteed small loss to prevent a large, possibly devastating loss. An insurer is a company selling the _____; an insured or policyholder is the person or entity buying the _____.
    a. Insurance
    b. ACCRA Cost of Living Index
    c. AD-IA Model
    d. ACEA agreement

Chapter 13. Rules versus Discretion—Can Policymakers Stick to Their Promises?

13. The _____ is an international organization of central banks which 'fosters international monetary and financial cooperation and serves as a bank for central banks.' It is not accountable to any national government. The BIS carries out its work through subcommittees, the secretariats it hosts, and through its annual General Meeting of all members. It also provides banking services, but only to central banks, or to international organizations like itself.

   a. 100-year flood
   b. 130-30 fund
   c. 1921 recession
   d. Bank for International Settlements

14. _____ is the practice within the banking industry of authorizing electronic transactions done with a debit card or credit card and holding this balance as unavailable either until the merchant clears the transaction _____ s can fall off the account anywhere from 1-5 days after the transaction date depending on the bank's policy; in the case of credit cards, holds may last as long as 30 days, depending on the issuing bank.

Signature-based credit and debit card transactions are a two-step process, consisting of an authorization and a settlement.

When a merchant swipes a customer's credit card, the credit card terminal connects to the merchant's acquirer which verifies that the customer's account is valid and that sufficient funds are available to cover the transaction's cost.

   a. Interbank network
   b. Electronic funds transfer
   c. Issuing bank
   d. Authorization hold

15. An economic and _____ is a single market with a common currency. It is to be distinguished from a mere currency union, which does not involve a single market. This is the fifth stage of economic integration.

   a. Commercial invoice
   b. Monetary union
   c. Customs union
   d. Free trade zone

16. _____ is money accepted for exchange of goods in an economy. The prevalence of one money over another arises, usually, when a government designates through decrees that the government shall accept only particular notes and coins in payment for taxes. Typically, money of _____ consists of stamped coins and minted paper bills.

Chapter 13. Rules versus Discretion—Can Policymakers Stick to Their Promises?

a. Local currency
b. Totnes pound
c. Currency
d. Security thread

17. A _____ or a flexible exchange rate is a type of exchange rate regime wherein a currency's value is allowed to fluctuate according to the foreign exchange market. A currency that uses a _____ is known as a floating currency. The opposite of a _____ is a fixed exchange rate.
   a. Floating exchange rate
   b. Floating currency
   c. Foreign exchange market
   d. Trade Weighted US dollar Index

18. Economics:

   - _____, the desire to own something and the ability to pay for it
   - _____ curve, a graphic representation of a _____ schedule
   - _____ deposit, the money in checking accounts
   - _____ pull theory, the theory that inflation occurs when _____ for goods and services exceeds existing supplies
   - _____ schedule, a table that lists the quantity of a good a person will buy it each different price
   - _____ side economics, the school of economics at believes government spending and tax cuts open economy by raising _____

   a. Variability
   b. McKesson ' Robbins scandal
   c. Demand
   d. Production

19. In finance, the _____s between two currencies specifies how much one currency is worth in terms of the other. It is the value of a foreign natione;s currency in terms of the home natione;s currency. For example an _____ of 102 Japanese yen to the United States dollar means that JPY 102 is worth the same as USD 1.
   a. ACCRA Cost of Living Index
   b. ACEA agreement
   c. Exchange rate
   d. Interbank market

Chapter 13. Rules versus Discretion—Can Policymakers Stick to Their Promises?

20. _____ is sometimes referred to as _____, actually it means Economic Monetary Union.

First ideas of an economic and monetary union in Europe were raised well before establishing the European Communities. For example, already in the League of Nations, Gustav Stresemann asked in 1929 for a European currency (Link) against the background of an increased economic division due to a number of new nation states in Europe after WWI.

a. European Monetary Union
b. Exchange rate mechanism
c. Euro Interbank Offered Rate
d. European Monetary System

21. The _____ is one of the world's most important central banks, responsible for monetary policy covering the 16 member States of the Eurozone. It was established by the European Union (EU) in 1998 with its headquarters in Frankfurt, Germany.

The predecessor to the _____ was the European Monetary Institute .

a. ACEA agreement
b. AD-IA Model
c. European Central Bank
d. ACCRA Cost of Living Index

Chapter 14. Dealing with Financial Crises—Does

1. In finance, a _____ is a debt security, in which the authorized issuer owes the holders a debt and, depending on the terms of the _____, is obliged to pay interest (the coupon) and/or to repay the principal at a later date, termed maturity. A _____ is a formal contract to repay borrowed money with interest at fixed intervals.

   Thus a _____ is like a loan: the issuer is the borrower (debtor), the holder is the lender (creditor), and the coupon is the interest.

   a. Prize Bond
   b. Zero-coupon
   c. Callable
   d. Bond

2. _____ refers to the movement of cash into or out of a business or financial product. It is usually measured during a specified, finite period of time. Measurement of _____ can be used

   - to determine a project's rate of return or value. The time of _____s into and out of projects are used as inputs in financial models such as internal rate of return, and net present value.
   - to determine problems with a business's liquidity. Being profitable does not necessarily mean being liquid. A company can fail because of a shortage of cash, even while profitable.
   - as an alternate measure of a business's profits when it is believed that accrual accounting concepts do not represent economic realities. For example, a company may be notionally profitable but generating little operational cash (as may be the case for a company that barters its products rather than selling for cash.) In such a case, the company may be deriving additional operating cash by issuing shares evaluating default risk, re-investment requirements, etc.

   _____ is a generic term used differently depending on the context. It may be defined by users for their own purposes.

   a. Strip financing
   b. Second lien loan
   c. Restricted stock
   d. Cash flow

3. _____ in its classic form is defined as a company from one country making a physical investment into building a factory in another country. It is the establishment of an enterprise by a foreigner. Its definition can be extended to include investments made to acquire lasting interest in enterprises operating outside of the economy of the investor.
   a. Financial Stability Forum
   b. Non-governmental organization
   c. Foreign direct investment
   d. Federal Deposit Insurance Corporation

4. The phrase _____ refers to the aspect of corporate strategy, corporate finance and management dealing with the buying, selling and combining of different companies that can aid, finance, or help a growing company in a given industry grow rapidly without having to create another business entity.

An acquisition, also known as a takeover or a buyout, is the buying of one company (the 'target') by another. An acquisition may be friendly or hostile.

   a. Productive and unproductive labour
   b. Peace dividend
   c. Political economy
   d. Mergers and acquisitions

5. The term _____ is used to describe countries that have a high level of development according to some criteria. Which criteria, and which countries are classified as being developed, is a contentious issue and there is fierce debate about this. Economic criteria have tended to dominate discussions.
   a. 100-year flood
   b. Developed country
   c. Least Developed Countries
   d. Trillion dollar club

6. The phrase _____ and acquisitions refers to the aspect of corporate strategy, corporate finance and management dealing with the buying, selling and combining of different companies that can aid, finance, or help a growing company in a given industry grow rapidly without having to create another business entity.

An acquisition, also known as a takeover or a buyout, is the buying of one company (the 'target') by another. An acquisition may be friendly or hostile.

   a. Differential accumulation
   b. Political economy
   c. Peace dividend
   d. Mergers

7. _____s is the social science that studies the production, distribution, and consumption of goods and services. The term _____s comes from the Ancient Greek oá¼°κονομῖα from oá¼¶κος (oikos, 'house') + vĺŒμος (nomos, 'custom' or 'law'), hence 'rules of the house(hold)'. Current _____ models developed out of the broader field of political economy in the late 19th century, owing to a desire to use an empirical approach more akin to the physical sciences.

a. Opportunity cost
b. Energy economics
c. Economic
d. Inflation

8. _____ is the increase in the amount of the goods and services produced by an economy over time. It is conventionally measured as the percent rate of increase in real gross domestic product, or real GDP. Growth is usually calculated in real terms, i.e. inflation-adjusted terms, in order to net out the effect of inflation on the price of the goods and services produced.
a. AD-IA Model
b. ACEA agreement
c. ACCRA Cost of Living Index
d. Economic growth

9. In economics, a _____ is a mechanism that allows people to easily buy and sell (trade) financial securities (such as stocks and bonds), commodities (such as precious metals or agricultural goods), and other fungible items of value at low transaction costs and at prices that reflect the efficient-market hypothesis.

_____s have evolved significantly over several hundred years and are undergoing constant innovation to improve liquidity.

Both general markets (where many commodities are traded) and specialized markets (where only one commodity is traded) exist.

a. Convertible arbitrage
b. Financial market
c. Market anomaly
d. Noise trader

10. The term _____ is applied broadly to a variety of situations in which some financial institutions or assets suddenly lose a large part of their value. In the 19th and early 20th centuries, many financial crises were associated with banking panics, and many recessions coincided with these panics. Other situations that are often called financial crises include stock market crashes and the bursting of other financial bubbles, currency crises, and sovereign defaults.
a. Macroeconomics
b. Financial crisis
c. Co-operative economics
d. Market failure

Chapter 14. Dealing with Financial Crises—Does

11. The cost advantages of using _____ include:

    • Reconciling conflicting preferences of lenders and borrowers

    • Risk aversion- intermediaries help spread out and decrease the risks

    • Economies of scale- using _____ reduces the costs of lending and borrowing

    • Economies of scope- intermediaries concentrate on the demands of the lenders and borrowers and are able to enhance their products and services (use same inputs to produce different outputs)

_____ include:

    • Banks
    • Building societies
    • Credit unions
    • Financial advisers or brokers
    • Insurance companies
    • Collective investment schemes
    • Pension funds

Financial institutions (intermediaries) perform the vital role of bringing together those economic agents with surplus funds who want to lend, with those with a shortage of funds who want to borrow.

In doing this they offer the major benefits of maturity and risk transformation. It is possible for this to be done by direct contact between the ultimate borrowers, but there are major cost disadvantages of direct finance.

Indeed, one explanation of the existence of specialist _____ is that they have a related (cost) advantage in offering financial services, which not only enables them to make profit, but also raises the overall efficiency of the economy.

   a. SICAV
   b. Broker-dealer
   c. Collective investment scheme
   d. Financial intermediaries

12. In economics and finance, _____ represents passive holdings of securities such as foreign stocks, bonds none of which entails active management or control of the securities' issuer by the investor; where such control exists, it is known as foreign direct investment. Generally, this means the investor holds less than 10% of the total shares or less than the amount needed to hold the majority vote.

Some examples of _____ are:

- purchase of shares in a foreign company.
- purchase of bonds issued by a foreign government.
- acquisition of assets in a foreign country.

Factors affecting international _____:

- tax rates on interest or dividends (investors will normally prefer countries where the tax rates are relatively low)
- interest rates (money tends to flow to countries with high interest rates)
- exchange rates (foreign investors may be attracted if the local currency is expected to strengthen)

_____ is part of the capital account on the balance of payments statistics.

a. CAN SLIM
b. Fund administration
c. Retirement Compensation Arrangements
d. Portfolio investment

13. In economics, _____ is the monetary policy device that a country's government (i.e., sovereign power) uses to regulate the flows into and out of a country's capital account, i.e., the flows of investment-oriented money into and out of a country or currency. _____s have become more prominent in the years since the Clinton administration blessed the efforts of the world community to create the World Trade Organization (WTO), primarily because globalization has increased the acceleration of currency domain strength, in other words, giving some currencies utility far beyond their physical geographic boundaries.

One characteristic of developed economies is liquid debt markets.

a. Second-round effect
b. Shadow Open Market Committee
c. Money creation
d. Capital control

14. The _____ is an international organization that oversees the global financial system by following the macroeconomic policies of its member countries, in particular those with an impact on exchange rates and the balance of payments. It is an organization formed to stabilize international exchange rates and facilitate development. It also offers financial and technical assistance to its members, making it an international lender of last resort.

a. ACCRA Cost of Living Index
b. Office of Thrift Supervision
c. International Monetary Fund
d. ACEA agreement

15. _____ is a concept in international development, political economy and international relations and describes the use of conditions attached to a loan, debt relief, bilateral aid or membership of international organizations, typically by the international financial institutions, regional organizations or donor countries.

_____ is typically employed by the International Monetary Fund, the World Bank or a donor country with respect to loans, debt relief and financial aid. Conditionalities may involve relatively uncontroversial requirements to enhance aid effectiveness, such as anti-corruption measures, but they may involve highly controversial ones, such as austerity or the privatization of key public services, which may provoke strong political opposition in the recipient country.

a. Participatory rural appraisal
b. Conditionality
c. Sector-Wide Approach
d. Capacity Development

16. _____ are potential claims on the freely usable currencies of International Monetary Fund members. _____s have the ISO 4217 currency code XDR.

_____s are defined in terms of a basket of major currencies used in international trade and finance.

a. Bilateral Investment Treaty
b. Quota share
c. Metzler paradox
d. Special Drawing Rights

17. Economic _____ is defined as an excess distribution to any factor in a production process above that which is required to induce the factor into the process or any excess above that which is necessary to keep the factor in its current use..

Classical Factor _____ is primarily concerned with the fee paid for the use of fixed (e.g. natural) resources. The classical definition is expressed as any excess payment above that required to induce or provide for production.

a. 1921 recession
b. 100-year flood
c. 130-30 fund
d. Rent

18. The _____ is an international financial institution that provides financial and technical assistance to developing countries for development programs (e.g. bridges, roads, schools, etc.) with the stated goal of reducing poverty.

The _____ differs from the _____ Group, in that the _____ comprises only two institutions:

- International Bank for Reconstruction and Development (IBRD)
- International Development Association (IDA)

Whereas the latter incorporates these two in addition to three more:

- International Finance Corporation (IFC)
- Multilateral Investment Guarantee Agency (MIGA)
- International Centre for Settlement of Investment Disputes (ICSID)

John Maynard Keynes (right) represented the UK at the conference, and Harry Dexter White represented the US.

The _____ is one of two major financial institutions created as a result of the Bretton Woods Conference in 1944. The International Monetary Fund, a related but separate institution, is the second.

a. Financial costs of the 2003 Iraq War
b. World Bank
c. Bank-State-Branch
d. Flow to Equity-Approach

19. The term _____ is a neo-Latin word meaning 'before the event'. _____ is used most commonly in the commercial world, where results of a particular action, or series of actions, are forecast in advance. The opposite of _____ is ex-post.
a. AD-IA Model
b. ACEA agreement
c. ACCRA Cost of Living Index
d. Ex-ante

20. Founded in 1991, the _____ uses the tools of investment to help build market economies and democracies in 27 countries from central Europe to central Asia. Its mission was to support the formerly communist countries in the process of establishing their private sectors.

Headquartered in London, the EBRD is owned by 61 countries and two intergovernmental institutions.

a. AD-IA Model
b. ACCRA Cost of Living Index
c. European Bank for Reconstruction and Development
d. ACEA agreement

21. A _____ is the massive selling of a country's currency assets by both domestic and foreign investors. Countries that utilize a fixed exchange rate are more susceptible to a _____ than countries utilizing a floating exchange rate. This is because of the large amount of reserves necessary to hold the fixed exchange rate in place at that fixed level.

a. Speculative attack
b. 130-30 fund
c. 100-year flood
d. Currency crisis

22. _____ is the prospect that a party insulated from risk may behave differently from the way it would behave if it were fully exposed to the risk. In insurance, _____ that occurs without conscious or malicious action is called morale hazard.

_____ is related to information asymmetry, a situation in which one party in a transaction has more information than another.

a. Moral hazard
b. 100-year flood
c. 1921 recession
d. 130-30 fund

23. _____ is the corporate management term for the act of reorganizing the legal, ownership, operational or better organized for its present needs. Alternate reasons for restructing include a change of ownership or ownership structure, demerger repositioning debt _____ and financial _____.

a. Securitization
b. Restructuring
c. Market value
d. Forecast period

ANSWER KEY

Chapter 1
1. c 2. d 3. a 4. d 5. d 6. c 7. d 8. c 9. c 10. d
11. d 12. d 13. d 14. d 15. d 16. d 17. c 18. c 19. c 20. d
21. a 22. b 23. d 24. d 25. d 26. b 27. b 28. d 29. b 30. d
31. d 32. d

Chapter 2
1. a 2. d 3. a 4. a 5. a 6. d 7. c 8. a 9. d

Chapter 3
1. c 2. d 3. d 4. b 5. a 6. d 7. d 8. b 9. d 10. a
11. b 12. a 13. d 14. d 15. a 16. d 17. d 18. d 19. b 20. a
21. a 22. c 23. c 24. b 25. d 26. d 27. b 28. b 29. d 30. c
31. c 32. d

Chapter 4
1. d 2. b 3. b 4. d 5. c 6. d 7. b 8. c 9. d 10. b
11. d 12. d 13. d 14. a 15. c 16. d

Chapter 5
1. d 2. d 3. d 4. d 5. d 6. c 7. c 8. d 9. a 10. b
11. b 12. b 13. d 14. a 15. b 16. a 17. a 18. d 19. a 20. d
21. d 22. c 23. d 24. d 25. d 26. b

Chapter 6
1. d 2. b 3. b 4. a 5. d 6. d 7. b 8. d 9. c 10. a
11. a 12. b 13. d 14. c 15. d 16. b 17. d 18. d 19. b 20. a
21. a 22. d 23. a 24. a 25. d 26. d 27. d 28. b 29. a 30. a
31. d 32. d 33. d 34. b 35. d 36. d 37. b 38. d 39. d 40. d
41. a 42. c 43. d 44. a 45. a 46. b 47. c

Chapter 7
1. d 2. b 3. b 4. d 5. c 6. d 7. d 8. d 9. c 10. d
11. b 12. d 13. d 14. d 15. a 16. a 17. d 18. a 19. a 20. c
21. b 22. d 23. c 24. b 25. d 26. a 27. c 28. d 29. c 30. d
31. a 32. b 33. a 34. b 35. d

Chapter 8
1. d 2. d 3. d 4. d 5. d 6. d 7. d 8. d 9. d 10. d
11. d 12. b 13. d 14. b 15. b 16. a 17. b 18. d 19. d 20. c
21. d 22. c 23. d 24. d 25. c 26. d 27. d 28. c 29. a

Chapter 9

1. d	2. b	3. d	4. d	5. c	6. d	7. d	8. d	9. a	10. b
11. b	12. d	13. d	14. a	15. a	16. d	17. b	18. d	19. d	20. c
21. a	22. d	23. b	24. b	25. b	26. c	27. d	28. a	29. d	30. d
31. c	32. d	33. d	34. d	35. b	36. d	37. c	38. a	39. d	40. b
41. c	42. b	43. a	44. c	45. a	46. d	47. a	48. d	49. b	50. d
51. d									

Chapter 10

1. d	2. d	3. b	4. d	5. d	6. d	7. d	8. a	9. d	10. d
11. c	12. d	13. d	14. d	15. d	16. d	17. d	18. d	19. b	20. d
21. c	22. a	23. a	24. a	25. d					

Chapter 11

1. a	2. d	3. c	4. d	5. a	6. c	7. d	8. c	9. d	10. b
11. a	12. d	13. b	14. d	15. d	16. a	17. c	18. d	19. d	20. d
21. b	22. a	23. d	24. a	25. d	26. d	27. d	28. d	29. d	30. c
31. c	32. c	33. d	34. c	35. d	36. d				

Chapter 12

1. d	2. d	3. d	4. b	5. d	6. d	7. a	8. a	9. d	10. d
11. d	12. c	13. c	14. d	15. d	16. d	17. d	18. d	19. a	20. a
21. d	22. d	23. d	24. a	25. d	26. b				

Chapter 13

1. b	2. d	3. a	4. d	5. d	6. d	7. d	8. c	9. d	10. b
11. d	12. a	13. d	14. d	15. b	16. c	17. a	18. c	19. c	20. a
21. c									

Chapter 14

1. d	2. d	3. c	4. d	5. b	6. d	7. c	8. d	9. b	10. b
11. d	12. d	13. d	14. c	15. b	16. d	17. d	18. b	19. d	20. c
21. a	22. a	23. b							

www.ingramcontent.com/pod-product-compliance
Lightning Source LLC
Chambersburg PA
CBHW082044230426

43670CB00016B/2777